D1356675

It's Great to be Back on Terra Cotta!

It's Great to be Back on Terra Cotta!

Quirky Quotes about Travel and Transport

AUBREY MALONE

ILLUSTRATIONS BY
BRIAN FITZGERALD

The
History
Press

First published 2011

The History Press
The Mill, Brimscombe Port
Stroud, Gloucestershire, GL5 2QG
www.thehistorypress.co.uk

© Aubrey Malone, 2011

The right of Aubrey Malone to be identified as the Author
of this work has been asserted in accordance with the
Copyrights, Designs and Patents Act 1988.

British Library Cataloguing in Publication Data.
A catalogue record for this book is available from the British Library.

ISBN 978 0 7524 5894 6

Typesetting and origination by The History Press
Printed in Great Britain

CONTENTS

INTRODUCTION

Each manner of transport has its delights but also its frustrations, Okay, so there are no parking problems on the moon – well, not yet anyway – but making a journey today isn't as simple as it used to be when you just sat in your vehicle, put your foot on the accelerator and, after a reasonable amount of time, reached your destination.

Before the advance of technology we might have had more break-downs, but just because you're sitting in a state-of-the-art SUV doesn't mean you'll get where you want to go more quickly than in the days when you travelled at the speed of a penny farthing bicycle.

It might take you as long to go from your London apartment to Heathrow as it does to go from Heathrow to Paris. Aye, there's the rub. And what about lost luggage, gridlock, road rage, clamped cars, park-ing fines, robbery and the other thousand shocks that steel is heir to – even terrorism?

Every generation has its heartaches as well as its miracles. The *Titanic* was supposed to be unsinkable but it didn't even survive its maiden voyage. The motor car, on the other hand, was regarded as an eight-day wonder when it first made its dodgy strides down a street. And now, for many of us, it's like our second home, or even our first one.

The bottom line, as William Goldman once said in a somewhat dif-ferent context, is that nobody knows anything, Which is why collecting a set of quotations from beleaguered commuters is an ambiguous joy. Sadistic in one sense but oddly comforting too, because the more you read about the trials and tribulations of others in the same boat – or even plane – the more you realise that we've all been that soldier at some point of our lives, caught in the middle of nowhere with a flat tyre and no spare, or irked beyond belief at the driver in front of us going at approxi-mately 12mph on a road too narrow to overtake ... as we're on the way to that all-important job interview we just can't be late for – but are.

Henry Ford has a lot to answer for, to be sure. So have the Wright – Wrong? – brothers. Or anybody else who foolishly imagined that by

shortening the time it took to get somewhere he wouldn't in some way also shorten the traveller's life, Yes, dear reader, stress can do that to you on the M1, or even crossing the Atlantic under a cerulean blue sky.

Were we better on Shank's Mare? Maybe so, but if different modes of transport weren't invented then neither would the outraged, and often outrageously funny, pronouncements of the unpunctual, the unlucky, and the unhinged.

In other words, fasten your seatbelts for a bumpy ride.

WHAT IS A CAR?

A car is just a giant moving handbag. You don't have to carry groceries, dry cleaning or anything. You can have five pairs of shoes with you at all times!

CYNTHIA HEIMEL

Automobile: A gas-guzzling horse on wheels, source of mobility for the masses, status for status seekers, exhilaration for the restless and sudden death for the unwary. Progenitor of suburbs, shopping malls, motels, shopping malls, motels, traffic jams, 'Baby on Board' signs, drive-in funeral parlours and endless rivers of asphalt.

RICK BAYAN

The car has become an article of dress without which we would feel uncertain, unclad, and incomplete in the urban compound.

MARSHALL MCLUHAN

The automobile is the greatest catastrophe in the entire history of city architecture.

PHILIP JOHNSON

The wheel is nice, but let's face it: someone was eventually going to come up with it. The answering machine? Now that took real innovation.

PAULA POUNDSTONE

The automobile changed our dress, manners, social customs, vacation habits, the shape of our cities, consumer purchasing patterns … and positions in intercourse.

JOHN KEATS

To argue that a car is simply a means of conveyance is like arguing that Blenheim Palace is simply a house.
JEREMY CLARKSON

The car, the furniture, the wife, the children – everything has to be disposable. Because the main thing today is – shopping.

ARTHUR MILLER

Cars are better than public transport. You have your own company, your own temperature control, your own music. And you don't have to put up with dreadful human beings sitting alongside you.

STEVEN NORRIS

A Range Rover is like a country cottage on wheels.

JONATHAN GLANCEY

We give people a box in the suburbs. It's called a house, and every night they sit in it staring at another box. In the morning they run off to another box called an office, and at the weekends they get into another box, on wheels this time, and grope their way through endless traffic jams.

CAROLINE KELLY

The whole point of using your car to go to work is that you can listen to the radio station of your choice while picking your nose.

JEREMY CLARKSON

MEETING BY ACCIDENT

Nigel Mansell is a highly experienced driver with an unblemished record of accidents.

SAMANTHA COHEN

He's watching us from hospital with his injured knee.

MURRAY WALKER

The nice thing about a plane crashing at an air show is that they always have good footage of the actual crash.

GEORGE CARLIN

A cement mixer collided with a prison van on the Kingston bypass. Motorists are asked to be on the lookout for sixteen hardened criminals.

RONNIE CORBETT

Accidents never happen to men of genius.

JAMES JOYCE

It takes 7,860 nuts to assemble a motorcar, and just one drunken one to scatter it all over the road.

CYRIL FLETCHER

Quizmaster: Name something you often misplace in your car.
Contestant: The steering wheel.

FAMILY FEUD

I have an underwater camera just in case I crash my car into a river and at the last minute I see a photo opportunity.

MITCH HEDBERG

There used to be a rule of thumb in the old BBC radio newsroom that in terms of newsworthiness, 60,000 dead in floods in China equalled 90 dead in a hotel fire in Italy, or two Brits slightly injured in a car crash in Brittany.

JEREMY PAXMAN

I'd rather have a serious car crash than a serious cock rash.

FRANK SKINNER

When you drive to the supermarket, driving standards immediately deteriorate as soon as you enter the car park. This is to prepare you for the truly shocking standards of imbecilic fatheads doing dangerous harebrained manoeuvres with their trolleys.

GUY BROWNING

I had an accident with a magician. It wasn't my fault. The guy came out of nowhere. AUGGIE COOK

Q. How often do Jumbo jets crash?
A. Just the once FRED METCALF

Don't come out of the closet in a moving vehicle with your father.
BOY GEORGE

I see the car crash as a tremendous sexual event: a liberation of human and machine libido. J.G. BALLARD

'There's been an accident,' they said, 'Your servant's cut in half, he's dead.' 'Indeed,'said Mrs Jones, 'Now please, send me the half that's got my keys.' HARRY GRAHAM

What is better than presence of mind in a railway accident? Absence of body. PUNCH

My wife came home and told me she had some good news and some bad news about the car. I said, 'What's the good news?' She said, 'The airbag works.' ROY 'CHUBBY' BROWN

I never worry about the plane crashing. Remember: in the case of an accident, the pilot is always the first on the scene. MAX KAUFFMANN

I once got hit by a Volkswagen. I had to go to the hospital to have it removed.
PAT MCCORMICK

Boston's freeway system was clearly designed by a person who had spent his childhood crashing trains.
BILL BRYSON

They say that if two airplanes collide it's a near-miss. Bullshit, it's a near-hit. A collision is a near-miss.
GEORGE CARLIN

Every fresh accident on the railroads is an advantage and leads to an improvement. What we now want is an overturn that would kill a bishop, or at least a dean. This mode of conveyance would then become perfect.
SYDNEY SMITH

The biggest mistake Bill Clinton ever made was not getting Teddy Kennedy to drive Monica Lewinsky home.
DENIS LEARY

A friend of mine, married for twenty years, tells me he proposed to his wife in a parked car. Which only goes to show you that you can have a nasty accident in your car even when it's stationary.
EDWARD PHILLIPS

'Officer, I've just been knocked down by my friend.' 'What gear was he in?' 'The usual woolly jumper and Nike runners.'
LIAM O'MAHONY

My only solution to the problem of habitual accidents is for everybody to stay in bed all day. Even then there is always the chance that you will fall out.
ROBERT BENCHLEY

I always sit at the back end of a plane. You never hear of a plane backing into a mountain.
TOMMY COOPER

COME FLY WITH ME

I just came back from a pleasure trip. I took my mother-in-law to the airport.
                                                        HENNY YOUNGMAN

Air power may either end war or end civilisation.
                                                        WINSTON CHURCHILL

I once travelled to Adelaide on Emu Airlines. I was 5,000 feet up in the air when someone pointed out to me that emus can't fly.
                                                        BILLY CONNOLLY

I flew to the premiere of *That's Entertainment 2* with Fred Astaire, Gene Kelly and Donald O'Connor. Four hoofers all on the same trip. I turned to Astaire during the flight and said to him, 'Do you know if this plane crashes, Ken Berry will be the biggest song-and-dance man in America!'
                                                        BOBBY VAN

Any mother could perform the jobs of several air traffic controllers with ease.
                                                        LISA ALTHER

Air hostesses are getting more and more like your mum. One said to me, 'Finish your dinner, There are people starving on Air India.'
                                                        BOB MONKHOUSE

It wasn't the aeroplanes, it was beauty that killed the beast.
FINAL LINES OF *KING KONG*

The average airplane is sixteen years old. And so is the average airplane meal.
JOAN RIVERS

I believe you have His 'n' Hers planes in your private airport. If your Other Half comes home last, does she back it into the runway to give her a quick escape in the morning?
JONATHAN ROSS TO JOHN TRAVOLTA

On airplanes I'm usually told it's not possible for the left and right side of my body to sit together, so one half of me is in 11B and the other in 23E.
MARIAN KEYES

We turned left at Greenland.
RINGO STARR TO AN INTERVIEWER WHO ASKED HIM
HOW THE BEATLES FOUND AMERICA

I'm not afraid of flying, just crashing.
DUDLEY MOORE

Catherine Zeta-Jones once hired a private jet to fly from Los Angeles to an awards ceremony in New York because smoking was banned on major airlines.
FIONA CUMMINS

A man phoned the airport and asked the lady on the other end of the line how long it would take him to fly to Tokyo. 'Just a minute,' she said. 'Thank you!' he beamed, and hung up.
VINCENT CUTTER

I was on this really cheap airline. We didn't get a movie. The pilot just flew low over drive-in theatres.
RODNEY DANGERFIELD

An airplane is the only vehicle that's a phallic symbol and a womb symbol at the same time.
DICK CAVETT

My parents have been visiting me for a few days. I just dropped them off at the airport. They leave tomorrow.
MARGARET SMITH

Ernie: Look at all those people down there. They look like ants.
Eric: They are ants. We haven't taken off yet.
EXCHANGE BETWEEN ERIC MORECAMBE AND ERNIE WISE

Naomi Campbell takes enough transatlantic flights to have a hole in the ozone named after her.
AINGEALA FLANNERY

I understand that manufacturers of aircrafts stand behind every plane they sell. I'd be happier if they stood under them.
HAL ROACH

It is imperative when flying that you restrain any tendency toward the vividly imaginative. Although it may momentarily appear to be the case, it is not at all likely that the cabin is entirely inhabited by crying babies smoking inexpensive domestic cigars.
FRAN LEBOWITZ

What's the latest invention on Polish airplanes? Outside toilets.

INTERNET JOKE

I cannot get in and out of aircraft toilets, but on three and a half hour flights I can hold out.

LUCIANO PAVAROTTI

Jet lag isn't all bad. It's a great excuse to go out and get pure stocious, on the principle that if you're sick and psychotic with a hangover you won't notice the jet lag. Or if you were planning a nervous breakdown, now's your chance. You'll be feeling alienated and fearful anyway, so you might as well double up. And my own personal favourite: jet lag affords the perfect opportunity to eat guilt-free Toblerones at two in the morning. Your poor stomach is still on home time; it had to miss its breakfast and it's not best pleased that someone wants to deprive it of its lunch as well.

MARIAN KEYES

When you step off the plane in Dallas and enter the main terminal you're greeted by a huge sign that proudly proclaims, 'Welcome to Dallas. We haven't had an assassination in over thirty years'.

AL FRANKEN

I've just flown in from Mexico so my arms are very tired.

MAX BOYCE

Man is flying too fast for a world that is round. Soon he will catch up with himself in a great rear-end collision and he will never know that what hit him from behind was another man.

JAMES THURBER

At the airport they asked me if anybody I didn't know gave me anything. Even the people I do know don't give me anything.

GEORGE WALLACE

Recently, on a whim, I decided to turn forty-eight. Physically the only problem I've noticed is that I can no longer read anything printed in letters smaller than Shaquille O'Neal. Also, to read a document I have to hold it far from my face. More and more I find myself holding documents – this is awkward on airplanes – with my feet.

DAVE BARRY

How difficult can it be to fly a plane? I mean, John Travolta can do it.

GRAHAM CHAPMAN

I want to play for Ireland. I qualify because I flew on Aer Lingus once.

JIMMY GREAVES

I always felt as if my twenties were like waiting to board an aeroplane. I was in the departure lounge of who I really am. **GERI HALLIWELL**

Sometimes when I'm flying over the Alps I think, 'That's like all the cocaine I sniffed.' **ELTON JOHN**

It's great to be back on terra cotta.

JOHN PRESCOTT AFTER A FLIGHT

I love travel. I've been to almost as many places as my luggage.

BOB HOPE

SHIPSHAPE

The vast majority of passengers on a cruise liner are there against their will.
PETER TINNISWOOD

I attribute my long life to the fact that I cancelled my trip on the *Titanic*.
GEORGE BURNS

Seasickness comes in two stages. In the first you're afraid you're going to die. In the second, you're afraid you're not going to.
SANDY TOKSVIG

The transatlantic crossing was so rough, the only thing I could keep in my stomach was the first mate.
DOROTHY PARKER

Alex Higgins should have been here today but he was launching a ship in Belfast and they couldn't get him to let go of the bottle.
DENNIS TAYLOR

The new nuclear submarine we have now is the best. It stays under water for two years and only comes up to the surface so the crew can re-enlist.
DICK GREGORY

A luxury liner is really just a bad play surrounded by water.
CLIVE JAMES

The Navy's a very gentlemanly business. You fire at the horizon to sink a ship and then you pull people out of the water and say, 'Frightfully sorry, old chap.'
WILLIAM GOLDING

I have nothing to declare but my genius.
OSCAR WILDE AT CUSTOMS AFTER COMING
OFF A FERRY

I have nothing to declare but my penis.

BRENDAN BEHAN IN SIMILAR CIRCUMSTANCES

A ship is always referred to as 'She' because it costs so much to keep one in paint and powder.

CHESTER NIMITZ

A captain always goes down with his ship.
Or, in the case of a submarine, up with it.

SID CAESAR

You dream you are crossing the Channel
Tossing about in a steamer from Harwich
Which is something between
A large bathing machine
And a very small second class carriage.

W.S. GILBERT

An English gentleman is useful at a hunt ball, and invaluable in a ship-wreck.

PATRICK CAMPBELL

I'm so dumb that if I escaped the *Titanic*, I'd probably climb aboard the *Marie Celeste*.

DANNY CUMMINS

Often undecided whether to desert a sinking ship for one that might not float, he would make up his mind to sit on the wharf for a day.

LORD BEAVERBROOK ON LORD CURZON

The Irish Navy is the best in the world, every evening all the sailors cycle home for their tea.

BRENDAN BEHAN

My experience of ships is that on them one makes an interesting discovery about the world. One finds one can do without it completely.

MALCOLM BRADBURY

The last telegram sent from the *Titanic* was recently auctioned off. It said, 'Help – they won't stop playing Celine Dion's Titanic song. And then everyone killed themselves.

CONAN O'BRIEN

The longer the cruise, the older the passengers.   PEG BRACKEN

Changing political parties in Ireland is merely like changing the deck chairs on the *Titanic*.   GAY BYRNE

A friend of mine was afraid of flying so she went by boat – and a plane fell on it.   FRED METCALF

The most difficult things to photograph are dogs, babies, Method actors and motorboats.   ALFRED HITCHCOCK

There is nothing, absolutely nothing, half as much worth doing as simply messing about in boats.   KENNETH GRAHAME

It rains so much in Manchester, it's the only town in England with lifeboat drills on the buses.   LES DAWSON

They built a tunnel from England to France. The English drive on the left-hand side of the road and the French on the right, so that's one busy lane.   JOHN MENDOZA

PARKING THICKETS

For a while I didn't have a car, I had a helicopter. There was no place to park it so I just tied it to a lamp-post and left it running.

STEVEN WRIGHT

A family is a social unit where the father is concerned with parking space, the children with outer space, and the mother with closet space.

EVAN ESAR

To park your car in Soho costs 20p for three minutes. That's £4 an hour, which is more than the minimum wage. There are people working in McDonald's in Soho who can look out the window and see parking meters earning more than they are.

SIMON EVANS

A pessimist has been defined as a woman who doesn't think she'll be able to squeeze her car into an infinitesimal parking-space. An optimist is a man who thinks she won't try.

EDWARD PHILLIPS

You know it's time to go on a diet when you're standing next to your car and you get a ticket for double parking.

TOTIE FIELDS

A man walks into a bar holding an alligator under his arm. He asks the barman, 'Do you serve traffic wardens here?' 'Of course we do,' says the barman. 'Good,' says the man. 'Give me a whiskey, and I'll have a traffic warden for my alligator.'

RICKY TOMLINSON

If God had intended us to fly, he would have made more parking available at airports.

MICHAEL HARKNESS

All modern architects should be pulled down and re-developed as car parks.

SPIKE MILLIGAN

I went to court for a parking ticket. I pleaded insanity.
STEVEN WRIGHT

Nigel claims that his wife is the only person in the world who parks her car by ear.
PETER CAGNEY

There are three things in this world you can do nothing about: Getting AIDs, getting clamped, and running out of Chateau Lafite 45.
ALAN CLARK

We have to go through life with the quiet expectancy of a motorist parked on a double yellow line.
ROY CLARKE

In order to preserve the natural beauty of the countryside, parking space was made available for no more than 30,000 cars.
ALAN CLARK

No travel writer I've ever known has written about the importance of parking.
J.G. BALLARD

The other night I was leaving my Fitness Emporium when I saw this bloke stretched out on his back in the par park. 'Excuse me,' he said, 'I'm a little stiff from badminton.' I told him I didn't give a fish's tit where he came from.
JOE O'CONNOR

Always put 'Pay and Display' parking tickets upside down in the centre of your windscreen in the hope that the parking warden will crick his neck trying to read it.
VIZ

I just solved the parking problem. I bought a parked car.
HENNY YOUNGMAN

When I first lived in Washington, a friend told me that you could quite literally get away with murder there, but you couldn't get away with illegal parking.

GAVIN ESLER

God has reserved a special place in hell for traffic wardens.

MICHAEL HARKNESS

It's okay, we can walk to the kerb from here.

**WOODY ALLEN TO DIANE KEATON IN *ANNIE HALL*
AFTER SHE PARKED HER CAR BADLY**

Why do you have to pay someone £5 to look after your car so you won't get a £50 parking ticket as you go for a £2 cup of coffee?

JILL PORTER

WITH GOD ON OUR SIDE

Don't worry. That's just God taking your photograph.

BONO TO SOPHIA LOREN AFTER SHE WAS FRIGHTENED BY LIGHTNING ON A PLANE

If you die in an elevator, be sure to push the 'Up' button.

SAM LEVENSON

Flying is where I always re-discover my faith. All those prayers you learned as a child suddenly come in very useful on take-off, landing, and when turbulence rears its ugly head at 30,000 feet.

EAMONN HOLMES

What's the difference between a Jehovah's Witness and a Lada? It's easier to close the door on a Jehovah's Witness. **SIL FOX**

In 1988 when Pope John Paul 11 visited Peru, an American security company was asked to create a vehicle that could withstand a terrorist attack. Early designs included gun ports. These were, however, dismissed by the Vatican after it was decided that it wouldn't look good for the Pope to fight back.

NEW YORK TIMES

A special front row seat in Paradise was set aside by the authorities for the used car salesman who finally became so devout he no longer cheated on Sundays. **HENRY SPALDING**

When I am reincarnated I want to come back to this world as a mother who doesn't drive. **ERMA BOMBECK**

Railways and the Church have their critics, but both are the best ways of getting a man to his ultimate destination. **REVD W. AWDRY**

The word 'Morality', if we met it in the Bible, would surprise us as much as the word 'telephone' or 'motor car.'

GEORGE BERNARD SHAW

If God had intended us to fly, he'd never have given us railways.

MICHAEL FLANDERS

Basically my husband has two beliefs. He believes in God, and also that when the gas gauge is on empty he still has a quarter of a tank left.

RITA RUDNER

I knew I'd chosen the wrong airline when I noticed the airsick bag had The Lord's Prayer on it.

LES DAWSON

We were Pentecostal. When I was growing up we couldn't go to movies, we couldn't listen to rock music and we couldn't wear make-up. That's just a lightbulb and a car away from being Amish.

RENE HICKS

After September 11, some people credited God with ensuring that there were far fewer people than usual in the targeted buildings and the hijacked planes. But why didn't he simply tip off the FBI?

CATHY YOUNG

AT THE TRACK

When the lights go green, Nigel Mansell goes red.

FRANK WILLIAMS

Grand Prix racing is like balancing an egg on a spoon while shooting the rapids.

GRAHAM HILL

I don't want to kill myself struggling for seventh place.

JAMES HUNT

Into lap 53, the penultimate last lap but one.

MURRAY WALKER

Show me a good loser and I'll show you a loser.

PAUL NEWMAN

Can you imagine the amount of money the first successful woman in Formula One will make? She'll have endorsements coming out of every orifice.

JOHN INVERDALE

Michael Schumacher walks around with a face like a wet Monday morning.

MARTIN BRUNDLE

There's no retirement plan for moto-crossers.

THOMAS MCGUANE

Ayrton Senna has never accepted he could be overtaken.

ALAIN PROST

Rene Arnoux is a real whacko. He lacked the one essential quality of the modern racing driver: intelligence.

KEITH BOTSFORD

Murray-Walker: When did you become aware you had a puncture?
Damon Hill: When the tyre went down.

I hate the big time. I feel the loss of close friends. I have to have bouncers at my birthday parties now.

JAMES HUNT IN 1976

There are lots of 'ifs' in the motor racing world, and 'if' is a very long word.

MURRAY WALKER

I don't make mistakes. I make prophecies which are immediately proved wrong.

MURRAY WALKER

I don't get frightened when I'm driving because if I'm in a nasty situation I'm too busy working it out. When I sit at home and think what can happen, then I'm scared.

JAMES HUNT

Alain Prost looks more like a scrum-half than a Grand Prix driver.

NIGEL ROEBUCK

Nigel Mansell has about as much charisma as a damp spark plug.

ALAN HUBBARD

What is called the World Driver's Championship is in fact the Car Manufacturer's Championship. Drivers are becoming irrelevant.

JAMES HUNT IN 1979

The point of Formula One is to export lung cancer and emphysema to the impressionable youths of the Far East.

MATTHEW NORMAN

Did you hear about the Polish Grand Prix driver? He made 100 pit stops – four for fuel and the other 96 to ask directions.

INTERNET JOKE

Not too long ago I lay awake in bed and counted all the people I've known who died racing. After an hour I'd reached fifty-seven.

JACKIE STEWART

I'm in greater danger each time I drive my own car than in a Formula One race. On the track I have no cars coming towards me and I'm with experienced professional drivers who all know their limits.

STEFANO MODENA

They name streets after guys like Greg Biffle: One Way and Dead End.

TONY STEWART

You may find this difficult to believe, but winning isn't as easy as it looks.

RON DENNIS

As you look at the first four, the significant thing is that Alboretto is fifth.

MURRAY WALKER

COME BLOW YOUR HORN

I couldn't repair your brakes so I made the horn louder.

STEVEN WRIGHT

At the height of my fame I couldn't take the dog for a walk during rush hour because motorists would be so busy honking at me that they'd run up each other's backsides.

GEORGE BEST

I don't bother to honk at motorists in South Florida who almost kill me. Generally it's a bad idea to honk down here anyway, inasmuch as the South Florida motoring public is as heavily armed as Iraq, but not as peace-loving.

DAVE BARRY

A split second has been defined as the period of time between the traffic lights changing to green and the motorist behind you sounding his horn.

EDWARD PHILLIPS

NOTES FROM THE UNDERGROUND

A literary competition wickedly requested misleading advice for foreigners. A devilish one went, 'On entering the Underground train, it is the custom to shake hands with everyone present.'

ARTHUR MARSHALL

We're used to being packed like sardines in the Underground, but they should let us get our tails in before they close the doors.

READER'S DIGEST

I used to stand in the subway when it was crowded and try to look pregnant. It was the only way to get a seat.

BETTY COMDEN

No matter which tube train you're waiting for, the wrong one always comes first.

MILES KINGTON

Even crushed against his brother in the Tube, the average Englishman pretends desperately that he's alone.

GERMAINE GREER

There are two kinds of men on tubes: Those who blow their noses and then examine the results in a handkerchief, and those who blow their noses without exhibiting any such curiosity, simply replacing the handkerchief in the pocket.

KENNETH WILLIAMS

Burton and Taylor travel down to hell on a moving staircase, a journey enlivened by the writhing of intertwined torsos, at whom Mr Burton glances as if they were corset advertisements on the London underground.   *TIME* MAGAZINE ON *DR FAUSTUS* IN 1967

Saturday morning, although recurring at regular and well foreseen intervals, always seems to take this railway by surprise.

W.S. GILBERT ON THE METROPOLITAN LINE

A sign on the London Underground says 'Dogs Must Be Carried'. But I can never find one.   TOMMY COOPER

You sit beside a robot on the public transport system for an hour. Then their mobile phone rings and they turn into Santa Claus. This is the great sadness of modern 'civilisation'.   AUBERON WAUGH

Most motorists use roads rather than the Underground or railways.

STEPHEN BYERS

Wall Street is the only place that people ride to in a Rolls Royce to get advice from those who take the subway.   WARREN BUFFETT

There's a phrase which says when you're tired of London you're tired of life. This explains why people on the Underground generally look suicidal.

GUY BROWNING

THE 64-DOLLAR QUESTIONS

Did you ever notice that the people who tell you their entire life stories when you're sitting beside them on airplanes are the same people who grudge telling you what time the next flight is at once you get off?

STEWART WILSON

On a train, why do I always end up sitting next to the woman who's eating a fruit pie by sucking the filling out through the hole in the middle?

VICTORIA WOOD

It is a curious fact, but nobody is ever seasick on land.

JEROME K. JEROME

It's strange, isn't it? Stand in the middle of a library and go 'Aaaargh' and everyone just stares at you. But do the same thing on a plane and they all join in.

TOMMY COOPER

'This car,' said the salesman, 'runs so smoothly you can't feel it, so quietly you can't hear it, so perfectly you can't smell it, and so fast you can't see it.' 'Then how the hell do I know it's there?' the potential buyer enquired.

GEORGE COOTE

Why don't they make the whole plane out of that black box stuff?

STEVEN WRIGHT

Why are there no windows in the toilets of airplanes? To protect you from the most dedicated perverts on the planet, hanging off the wing to get a peep?

BILLY CONNOLLY

My favourite form of relaxation is wondering what happened to the number 10 bus.

ANNE-MARIE HOURIHANE

Why was the taxi driver not prosecuted for knocking down a pedestrian? Because he was walking at the time.   JUNE RODGERS

The pilot said, 'We're currently hurtling through the air at 500mph. Please feel free to move about.' Then you land. You're travelling at one mile per hour and you hear, 'You must remain seated for your safety.' I'm wondering: Can we take off again because I need my coat from the overhead.   CAROL LEIFER

I wonder if Watson's in the relaxed state of mind that he's in.   MURRAY WALKER

It takes two to make a one-way street.   OGDEN NASH

There are ways out of everything apart from the city of Oxford's one-way system.   SIMON MAYO

The great and recurrent question about abroad is: Is it worth getting there?   DAME ROSE MACAULAY

When I'm on a plane I can never get my seat to recline more than a couple of centimetres but the guy in front of me, his seat comes back far enough for me to do dental work on him.

ELLEN DeGENERES

PUTTING THINGS IN TRAIN

My father used to be a train driver. He got the sack for overtaking.

SPIKE MILLIGAN

Motoring is a fearfully wrong way of seeing the country, but an awfully nice way of doing without railway trains.

AUGUSTUS JOHN

Railway timetables may be found in public libraries filed under 'Fiction'.

NIGEL REES

Nowadays a train driver's day is a timetable of sandwiches and Sudoku. It's like being unemployed except you have to go to work.

JACK DEE

Men build bridges and throw railroads across deserts, and yet they contend that the job of sewing on a button is beyond them. Accordingly, they don't have to sew buttons.

HEYWOOD BROUN

The only way to buy a railway ticket in advance is to go online and spend three hours entering approximately 900 details of your proposed journey, including preferred width of track and whether you have a nut allergy.

BILL BRYSON

The world's worst train robbery is what they charge for a hamburger in the dining car.

LEOPOLD FECHTNER

I'm not a fan of the modern railway system. I strongly object to paying £27.50 to walk the length of the train with a sausage in a plastic box.

VICTORIA WOOD

Trains are the most civilised, comfortable, romantic and therefore obsolescent means of public transport.

RICK BAYAN

Q. Does this train stop at Brighton?

A. I hope so or there's going to be a hell of a splash.

KENNY EVERETT

The whistle shrilled and in a moment I was chugging out of Grand Central's dreaming spires, followed only by the anguished cries of relatives who would now have to go to work. I had chugged only a few feet when I realised that I had left without the train so I had to run back and wait for it to start.

S.J. PERELMAN

I still have two abiding passions. One is my model railway, the other, women. But at the age of eighty-nine I find I'm getting just a little too old for model railways.

PIERRE MONTEUX

On Sunday I took a train, which didn't seem to want to go there, to Newcastle.

J.B. PRIESTLY

The journey from Carmarthen to Aberystwyth by train is one of the most reposeful stretches of railed track on earth. The railway company has a contract with the bees. They don't molest the passengers or try to scrounge free rides. The trains in return do not disturb the pollen.

GWYN THOMAS

Uncool people never hurt anybody. All they do is collect stamps, read science fiction books and stand on the end of railway platforms staring at trains.

BEN ELTON

Whoever said 'It's better to travel than to arrive' should get his head examined. To travel is awful and to arrive lovely. The only time it's not entirely unbearable to travel is when you're on the *Orient Express*, and your daily champagne allowance would fell an elephant.

MARIAN KEYES

Margaret Thatcher sounds like the Book of Revelation read out over a railway station public address system by a headmistress of a certain age wearing calico knickers.   **CLIVE JAMES**

Some people like to travel by train because it combines the slowness of a car with the cramped public exposure of an airplane.   **DENNIS MILLER**

RKO Studios was the biggest electric train set any boy ever had.   **ORSON WELLES**

To our dismay a rare thing happened – our train was punctual.   **JAN GORDON**

Going to work for a large company is like getting on a train. Are you going 60mph or is the train going 60mph and you're just sitting still?   **PAUL GETTY**

Did you hear about the Polish railway gate attendant who left the gate ajar because he was half expecting a train?   **INTERNET JOKE**

I never travel without my diary. One should always have something sensational to read on the train.   **OSCAR WILDE**

Muddled old gentleman to railway porter, 'Could you please tell me if this train claps at Stopham junction?'   **ARTHUR MARSHALL**

Passengers Hit By Cancelled Trains.   **NEWSPAPER HEADLINE**

My heart aches and a drowsy numbness drains my sense, as though of hemlock I had drunk. Signed: a British Rail tea victim.   **MARGARET ETHERIDGE**

We're often told in our newspapers that England is disgraced by this and that, by the wretchedness of our army, by the unfitness of our navy, by the immobility of our prejudices and whatnot; but the real disgrace of England is the railway sandwich.   **ANTHONY TROLLOPE**

The train now standing on Platform 3 will, we hope, in due course be moved back on to the lines. Will the passengers who've taken the 4.15 train from Platform 8 to Ponders End please bring it back again at once. **RICHARD MURDOCH**

Daphne Dolores Moorhead had a figure as full of curves as a scenic railway. **P.G. WODEHOUSE**

The Aberystwyth Cliff Railway is the train you take when your life has gone wrong. It creeps up the hill at the speed of lichen. You get off at the top, fortify yourself from a Styrofoam cup with tea the colour and strength of a horse, and walk to Clarach. **MALCOLM PRYCE**

I doubt that art needed Ruskin any more than a moving train needs one of its passengers to shove it. **TOM STOPPARD**

A commuter is one who spends his life
In riding to and from his wife.
A man who shaves and takes a train,
And then rides back to shave again. **E.B. WHITE**

I have seldom heard a train go by and not wished I was on it. Those whistles sing bewitchment. Railways are irresistible bazaars, snaking along perfectly level no matter what the landscape, improving your mood with speed and never upsetting your drink. **PAUL THEROUX**

In Darlington the shops seemed to be full of nothing but postcards of a great train crash that had occurred there. **ROBERT MORLEY**

MODEL BEHAVIOUR

Ford and Microsoft are getting together so you can buy a car online. However, note this. If you order a Ford on your computer and the computer crashes, the car will also explode. **BILL MAHER**

Women are just like cars. If you want a nice comfortable ride you go for a Merc. If you want something very sexy but awkward you go for a Ferrari. If you want something easy to park you go for a Cinquecento. **EDDIE IRVINE**

Like a Volvo, Bjorn Borg is rugged, has good after sales service, and is very dull. **CLIVE JAMES**

One enjoys the cheek of a car company that can take a panelled sitting-room, propel it down the road at over 100mph and still make as little noise as a skilled fly fisherman eating his packed lunch. **JOHN WHISTON ON THE ROLLS-ROYCE**

I intended to buy a Chevy but I couldn't tell the difference between the genuine one and all those counterfeit Chevys out there, so I bought a Ford. **DON CHARLESTON**

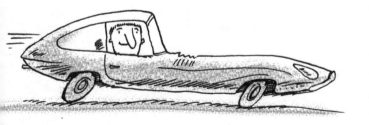

I had a lady for elocution who said to me, 'Gerry, voices are like cars. They can range from a Mercedes down to a Morris Minor – and you've got a Morris Minor.'   FR GERRY MOLONEY

There are two ways of inducing a bout of vomiting. You can stick a couple of fingers down your throat or you can look at a Celica.

JEREMY CLARKSON

I am a Ford, not a Lincoln.   GERALD FORD

My father told me that if I saw a man in a Rolls-Royce you could be sure he wasn't a gentleman unless he was a chauffeur.

EARL OF ARRAN

My sister bought a new car with a global positioning device so she never gets lost. Unfortunately it's the Republican model and it won't let her turn left.   DARYL HOGUE

There are a couple of mechanical devices which increase sexual arousal in women. Chief among these is the Mercedes-Benz 380SL convertible.   P.J. O'ROURKE

Jaguar recalled 3,500 cars but they were quick to point out that the problem was strictly with emissions and nothing to do with the vehicle's main function – getting bald, middle-aged guys laid.

BILL MAHER

The Vauxhall 30-98 had great long con-rods that rose majestically and sank again, lolloping with easy leisure and dipping into the oil. When you started her up she used to say, 'Guddugety-Guddugety-Gonk, Guddugety-Guddugety-Gonk.' She'd speak like no other motor car unless it was one of W.O. Bentley's majestic green monsters who would civilly reply, 'Berdoobeiy-Berdoobely-Bonk, Berdoobley-Berdoobley-Bonk'.
                                                                WILLIAM CONNOR

A new addition has been added to the Dean family, I got a red '53 MG – milled head, hot engine. My sex pours itself into fat curves, broadslides and broodings, drags, etc. You have plenty of competition. I have been sleeping with my MG. We make it together, honey.
                                    JAMES DEAN IN A LETTER TO HIS GIRLFRIEND
                                                            BARBARA GLENN

The E-type jag was the great British phallic symbol. It was memorable for featuring heavily in the opening credits of the *Simon Dee Show*. Since then, however, most of them have rusted away.
                                                            CHRISTY CAMPBELL

The best way for a guy to impress a girl at the gym is with pull-ups. Pull up in a Corvette, pull up in a Rolls-Royce, pull up in a Cadillac …
                                                            CONAN O'BRIEN

I bought my wife a little Italian car called a Mafia. It has a hood under the hood.   HENNY YOUNGMAN

If you stay in Beverly Hills too long you become a Mercedes.
                                                            DUSTIN HOFFMAN

On his fiftieth wedding anniversary Henry Ford was asked the formula for a successful marriage. He replied that it was the same formula that had made the motor car successful: 'Stick to the same model.'
                                                            JAMES SIMPSON

My brother gave me his Pinto but he neglected to tell me one thing: It doesn't handle well on pavement.   CHRISTINE CROSBY

Pauper: I hear you got a new Rolls. What happened to the one you bought last month?
Millionaire: The ashtrays were full.   INTERNET JOKE

Your professional golfer takes longer to line up a six-foot putt than the Toyota corporation takes to turn raw iron ore into a Corolla.
                                                            DAVE BARRY

With two in the front and two in the back, the Mini can fit into the most cramped spaces. It looks better on those with skinny legs.
                                                            CRAIG BROWN

Women are like cars. We all want a Ferrari but we end up with a station wagon.   TIM ALLEN

SPEED MERCHANTS

For over twenty years virtually everybody in the United States has been violating the speed limit except for Ralph Nader and elderly people wearing hats.   DAVE BARRY

If there's one day in the year when you know it's perfectly safe to break any speed limit you like and drive around completely pissed, it's Christmas Day; not a guard in sight – principally because most of them are too pissed to drive themselves, having spent the day lashing into the bottles all the businesses in the locality dropped in to them as thank yous for the previous year's vigilance.   DONAL RUANE

On your average weekday there are two types of car drivers on Britain's motorways. There are pensioners visiting other pensioners and there are sales reps who have three calls to make in a day and 500 miles between them. If you suddenly find yourself being flashed by a car so close behind you that you can see the drivers' nostril hair you can be fairly sure that it isn't a pensioner in a desperate rush to visit another pensioner.   GUY BROWNING

Drive like hell and you'll get there.

GRAFFITI

Middle age is when you're more worried about how long your car will last instead of how fast it'll go.

EDDIE IRVINE

A poll showed 14 per cent of men have received oral sex while driving. They must be the same 14 per cent who are deathly afraid of speed bumps.

CONAN O'BRIEN

Giles Villeneuve did everything in his life at 200mph: skiing, driving the speedboat, playing backgammon …

PATRICK TAMBAY

The freeway is where drivers under 25 do over 90, and drivers over 90 do 25.

GEORGE COOTE

It's impossible to travel faster than the speed of light, and certainly not desirable. One's hat keeps blowing off.

WOODY ALLEN

GET ON THE BUS

Definition of a school bus driver: Someone who thought he liked the company of children. **HAL ROACH**

My mum and dad are both dead now and I think of some of the things I wish I'd said to them, like 'Be careful of that bus.' **KEVIN GILDEA**

I only respect horoscopes that are specific: 'Today Neil Perelman, wearing tight-fitting wool knickers, will kill you on the cross-town bus.' **GEORGE CARLIN**

Anyone can be 52, but it takes a bus to be a 52A. **SPIKE MILLIGAN**

After meeting Robin Williams you feel as if you've been hit by a bus. **SARAH CADEN**

You know what it's like in a crowded bus, going through twelve pockets for your fare, with two parcels in your teeth. **BASIL BOOTHROYD**

Sometimes I'm sitting on a bus and I see somebody I know strolling along the pavement. We both wave to one another and the bus moves on. Then it stops at traffic lights and you can sense the person catching up. You think: 'Oh God, now I've got to wave again.' So you both do a second self-conscious kind of wave and the bus moves on again. Now you're stuck in traffic again and thinking, 'I just couldn't face a third one. Come on, bus, move. Here he comes again.' I want a few big major chronic stresses. It's little ones like those that have me wrecked. **PAT INGOLDSBY**

You know you're poor when you envy people with bus passes. **BONNIE McFARLANE**

When a minority wants something that is deeply offensive to a majority, it must be told to bugger off. This is why every one of London's 5,000 buses should be burned and their drivers put to death.

JEREMY CLARKSON

I never run for the bus.

LINFORD CHRISTIE

The English don't speak unless they have something to say, which is very confusing. I spent a long time trying to chat to people at London bus stops about the weather, the frequency of buses, the state of the country and the future of mankind. In England they don't do that. They thought I was from a home for the bewildered and moved away from me.

MAEVE BINCHY

She couldn't edit a bus ticket.

KELVIN MACKENZIE AFTER HEARING THAT JANET STREET-PORTER HAD BEEN
CHOSEN AS EDITOR OF *THE INDEPENDENT ON SUNDAY* IN 1999

The guy in front of me on the bus went into convulsions. He was sweating and puking and almost swallowed his tongue. His friend told me he'd been drinking for fifty-five days straight. We finally got him off the bus and I thought: Great. Now who's going to drive?

KATHLEEN MADIGAN

Art has to move you and design does not, except if it's a good design for a bus.

DAVID HOCKNEY

I felt guilty for wearing high shoes. A tiny invisible feminist sat on my shoulder, mocking. 'Look at you, pandering to men. See how your high heels make you walk with a wiggle.' When actually it was only because I was five foot one and wanted to see the number of my bus over people's heads.

MARIAN KEYES

A sexual fantasy may be described as anything from the plundering of Brigitte Bardot to the successful pursuit of a one-legged bus conductress, consummated on the stairway of a Number 11 bus hurtling along the Kings Road.

ROBERT MORLEY

There once was a man who said 'Damn'
It is borne upon me that I am
An engine that moves
In determinate grooves
I'm not even a bus, I'm a tram.

MAURICE EVAN HARE

Dublin Bus has been taking out newspaper ads saying that all services would 'operate normally' today. That's what I'm afraid of.

PETER HOWICK

Interviewer: What would happen if Mrs Thatcher was run over by a bus?

Lord Carrington: It wouldn't dare.

EXCHANGE DURING THE FALKLANDS WAR

Readers under thirty-five may not know what a trolleybus looked like. They were electric buses powered by overhead lines like trams. They were swift, roomy and gave off no fumes … so London Transport got rid of them.

MICHAEL GREEN

Russia scares me. The people on the buses are so serious they look like they're going to the electric chair.

MUHAMMAD ALI

What is this that roareth thus?
Can it be a Motor Bus?
Yes, the smell and hideous hum
Indicate Motorem Bum.
Domine, defende nos
Contra hos Motores Bos!

ALFRED GODLEY

I'm a retired Christian with a capital C. All I believe is that a No.11 bus goes along the Strand to Hammersmith. But I know it isn't being driven by Santa Claus.

PETER O'TOOLE

If you want to understand democracy, spend less time in the library with Plato and more time in the buses with people.

SIMEON STRUNSKY

This omnibus business is not what it is reported to be. I hailed one at the bottom of Whitehall and told the man to take me to Carlton House Terrace. But the fellow flatly refused.

GEORGE CURZON

Anybody seen in a bus over the age of thirty has been a failure in life.

DUCHESS OF WESTMINSTER

I've always wanted to date a man who travels and dreams do come true. I'm now seeing a bus driver.

JULIE KIDD

There's one statesman of the present day of whom I always say: He would have escaped making the blunders he's made if he had only ridden more in omnibuses.

SIR ARTHUR HELPS

Aunt Jane observed the second time
She tumbled off a bus
'The step is short from the sublime
To the ridiculous'.

HARRY GRAHAM

There aren't any good brave causes left. If the big bang does come and we all get killed off it won't be in aid of the old-fashioned, grand design. It'll just be for the Brave New nothing-very-much-thank-you. About as pointless and inglorious as stepping in front of a bus.

JOHN OSBORNE

I don't understand bus lanes. Why are poor people allowed to get where they're going faster than me?　**JEREMY CLARKSON**

LA bus drivers are striking. They want a big raise – and in exact change.　**JAY LENO**

As a frequent visitor to Ireland from Canada, I admire the way the Writer's Museum celebrates the work of the masters of Irish fiction. To their ranks should be added the name of whoever produces the timetables that adorn Dublin bus stops.

EDWARD BARBER

LEGAL EAGLES

Police Officer to Teenager: How long have you been driving?
Teenager: Not long, just three trees, two lamp-posts and one pedestrian.

EDWARD PHILLIPS

I stopped drinking because I had a problem. I'd get pulled over by the cops and start dancing to their lights thinking I'd made it to another club.

BILL HICKS

Policeman to motorist: Excuse me, sir, a lady claiming to be your wife fell out of the car a few miles back.
Motorist: Thank God, I thought I'd gone deaf.

INTERNET JOKE

Policeman: What are you doing lying in the gutter – were you knocked down?
Man: No, I just found this parking space so I sent my wife out to buy a car.

FRED METCALF

'I presume you don't intend to drive that vehicle,' the angry policeman said to the inebriated Irishman about to climb into his car. 'You hardly expect me to actually *walk* home in this condition!' the Irishman replied.

JACK CRUISE

I'd like to see speed limits that take into account what song you're listening to on the radio. Ideally if a police car pulled you over for doing, say, 95mph in a 75 zone and you could prove to him that you were listening to the Isley Brothers' version of 'Twist and Shout', he would not only have to let you off, but he would also be required by law to sing along with you.

DAVE BARRY

The worst drug by a mile is the common or garden sleeping pill. I tried one once on a flight from Beijing to Paris and was so removed from anything you might call reality that to this day I have no recollection of the emergency landing we made in Sharjah. I would like to see a law imposed whereby anyone who takes a prescription for sleeping pills is forced to hand over their driving licence. And their children.

JEREMY CLARKSON

A cop pulled me over and told me I could only go one way down this street. 'I AM only going one way,' I said. He said, 'Did you not see the arrows?' I said, 'I didn't even see the damn Indians.'

RODNEY DANGERFIELD

Policeman: What are you doing in there?
Motorist: Just necking, officer.
Policeman: Well put your neck back in your trousers now and move on.

BRIAN BUTLER

Traffic Cop: Do you know you were doing over 100 kilometres an hour?
Driver: Impossible. I only left home twenty minutes ago.

GEORGE COOTE

Policeman to blonde: Why didn't you stop when I waved at you?
Blonde: I'm not that kind of girl.

EDWARD PHILLIPS

DUH!

Airplanes are interesting toys but of no military value.

FERDINAND FOCH

You need reasonably good sight to be in the Navy but once you've flown a bit as a pilot you can usually guess the way.

PRINCE ANDREW

A fella asked me recently if I'd found my karma. 'No,' I said, 'but how much does it cost and how far can it go?'

DAVID FEHERTY

So tell us all about Europe? What movie did they show on the plane?

CHRISTINE BARANSKI

Nigel Mansell is the last person in the race apart from the five in front of him.

MURRAY WALKER

Neddie Seagoon: You're back early.
Henry Crun: Yes, we brought the train back on the aeroplane.

SPIKE MILLIGAN'S *GOON SHOW*

The traffic is very heavy at the moment so if you're thinking of leaving now you should set off a few minutes earlier.

RADIO BROADCAST

For the first time in fifty years, bus passenger numbers have risen to their highest level ever.

JOHN PRESCOTT

The guy who invented the first wheel was an idiot. The genius was the guy who invented the other three.

SID CAESAR

At last a smile from Jacques Villeneuve to match his bleached hair.

JONATHAN LEDGARD

Last year I took the wife on a world cruise. This year she says she wants to go somewhere else.

LES DAWSON

Mansell is taking it easy. Oh no he isn't – it's a lap record.

MURRAY WALKER

Greg Strange needs no introduction. He's motoring correspondent for LBC.

CAROL THATCHER

He's completely unoverawed by Senna.

JAMES HUNT

Do my eyes deceive me or is Senna's car sounding a bit rough?

MURRAY WALKER

Denis Norden thought that Johann Strauss's car would have been registered as 123, 123.

STEVE RACE

Patrick Tambay's hopes, which were nil before, are absolutely zero now.

MURRAY WALKER

Upon ringing a restaurant to ask if they had wheelchair access, I was told that they accepted all major credit cards.

PAT FITZPATRICK

Renault are currently enjoying huge losses.

GREG STRANGE

Motorist:	Can I insure my car against fire?
Insurance Agent:	Yes, but why not insure it against theft too.
Motorist:	That would be mad. Who'd bother stealing a burning car? **EDWARD PHILLIPS**

I can't swim. I can't drive either. I was going to learn to drive but then I thought: What if I crash into a lake? **DYLAN MORAN**

Mansell, Senna, Prost. Put them in any order and you end up with the same three drivers. **DEREK WARWICK**

He said to the travel agent, 'I want a round-the-world ticket'. 'One way?' she asked. **GEORGE COOTE**

For years I thought 'in loco parentis' meant 'My dad's an engine driver'. **BOB MONKHOUSE**

With the race half gone, there's still half the race to go. **MURRAY WALKER**

Airplanes may kill you, but they ain't likely to hurt you. **SATCHEL PAIGE**

This would have been Senna's third win in a row had he won the two before. **MURRAY WALKER**

Most cars on our roads have only one occupant, usually the driver. **CAROL MALIA**

I'll never have a baby because I'm afraid I'd leave it on the top of the car. **LIZ WINSTEAD**

Either that car is stationary or it's on the move. **MURRAY WALKER**

Trees cause more pollution than cars. **RONALD REAGAN**

I always wanted to travel overseas to places like Canada. **BRITNEY SPEARS**

POETIC LICENCE

One of my favourite pastimes is listening to poetry on cassette in the car while driving. God help the poor sod who steals my car and cranks up the stereo to get Ezra Pound at full tilt.　　**SIMON ARMITAGE**

I find driving a wonderful time for drifting into composition or revision. if it's iambic pentameter I count it on the steering wheel.

SEAMUS HEANEY

When I started writing poetry I believed there was something wrong with putting the word 'motor car' in a line.　　**DERMOT BOLGER**

Language is like a car able to go 200mph but which is restricted by the traffic laws of prose to a reasonable speed. Poets are fond of accelerating.　　**KENNETH KOCH**

Poets are known for being non-drivers, and it seems that many also have difficulty using their answering machines – not to mention speaking into other people's.　　**JAMES CAMPBELL**

Writing is like jumping from a plane. The worrying thing is that you don't know if you're going to come out with a parachute or a grand piano.

JOE O'CONNOR

Like minor poets, traffic wardens feel that anything they've written down, like the first two digits of your number plate or the date, are too precious to be crossed out.　　**CLEMENT FREUD**

It is unfortunate that most travel books are written by people whose only talent is for travel.　　**JOHN BRODERICK**

Certain places seem to exist mainly because someone has written about them.
                                                        JOAN DIDION

Writing is like driving at night in the fog. You can only see as far as your headlights, but you can make the whole trip that way.
                                                        E.L. DOCTOROW

Americans like fat books and thin women.   RUSSELL BAKER

It must be beautiful if you cannot read.
                            GEORGE BERNARD SHAW ON THE NEON
                            LIGHTS OF BROADWAY AT NIGHT

In America only the successful writer is important. In France all writers are important, in England no writer is important, and in Australia you have to explain what a writer *is*.   GEOFFREY COTTEREL

CALL ME A TAXI

He asked me to call him a cab. I said, 'Hello, cab.'

DOROTHY PARKER

A good way of packing is to start with yourself naked and pretend that you're getting dressed. In this way you will systematically remember every article of clothing. The only drawback to this approach is if the taxi arrives half an hour early.

GUY BROWNING

To me the outdoors is what you must pass through in order to get from your apartment into a taxicab.

FRAN LEBOWITZ

One night a drunk man got into a taxi and said to the driver, 'Take me to the Gresham Hotel.' The driver said, 'This *is* the Gresham.' He got out, handed him £20 and said, 'Next time don't drive so fast.'

HAL ROACH

I jumped in a taxi the other day. I said, 'King Arthur's Close.' The driver said, 'Don't worry, I'll lose him at the next set of lights.'

TOMMY COOPER

The taxi drivers in San Francisco are wonderful. They obey no laws except those of gravity.

RAYMOND CHANDLER

It's a nightmare travelling in London at present. The other day I had to stand all the way from Marble Arch to Hammersmith. And I was in a taxi.

FRED METCALF

As the taxi driver dropped me at the House of Commons one day he said only two honest people had ever entered it – myself and Guy Fawkes.

BERNADETTE MCALISKEY

No nice men are good at getting taxis.   KATHARINE WHITEHORN

A hospital bed is a parked taxi with the meter running.

GROUCHO MARX

London cabbies spend years learning the street layout. In New York, cabbies learn which thermos is for coffee and which is for urine.

JON STEWART

Taxi-drivers are simply not to be trusted, usually because of a pronounced death-wish, a deeply dishonest approach to what remains of life here on earth, a refusal to activate the meter, and a latent intention to find a quiet spot in the suburbs to ditch your corpse, having removed clothes and valuables.

ROBERT MORLEY

An empty taxi arrived at 10 Downing Street and when the door was opened, Clement Attlee got out.   WINSTON CHURCHILL

The only people really keeping the spirit of irony alive in Australia are taxi-drivers and homosexuals.   BARRY HUMPHRIES

I phoned my local cab firm and said, 'Can you please send me a big fat racist bastard with a personal hygiene problem some time before I have my menopause?'

JO BRAND

Anyone who loves theme parks has to try a New York cab.

MICHAEL BARRYMORE

When I was making *Taxi Driver* I took out a cab licence to research the part. A passenger recognised me one day. He said, 'Times hard on the acting front, eh?'

ROBERT DE NIRO

When I go into taxis, the first thing they say is, 'Hello, Eric, I thought you were dead.'

ERIC SYKES

Clark Gable's ears make him look like a taxi-cab with both doors open.

HOWARD HUGHES

I have done almost every activity inside a taxi which does not require main drainage.

ALAN BRIEN

A BITE OF THE BIG APPLE

New York is the only city in the world where you can get deliberately run over on the sidewalk by a pedestrian.
Russell Baker

People say New Yorkers can't get along. Not true. I saw two complete strangers sharing a cab there. One took the tyres and the other guy got the engine.
David Letterman

When you get hit by a car in Brooklyn they don't call an ambulance. It's showtime.
Eddie Murphy

New York has 200 new portable toilets. They're yellow, have four wheels, and a driver with a weird name.
David Letterman

Horsedrawn carriages used to average 11½mph in New York's midtown traffic. The average speed of automobiles there now is about 6.
Norman Geddes

When you go to New York you notice that you need two hands to open a letterbox but you fly a plane with one.
George Mikes

New York is a nice place to visit if you're flying over it.
Zero Mostel

The New York Marathon is a reminder of the beauty of a sport in which a fiftysomething ordinary Joe can line up alongside a world champion. It's like a retired mother of three parking her Micra alongside Michael Schumacher on the grid in Monaco. Or a hacker joining Tiger Woods on the first tee of the US Open.
Shane Hegarty

Any time four New Yorkers get into a cab together without arguing, a bank robbery has just taken place.
Johnny Carson

Traffic signals in New York are just rough guidelines.

DAVID LETTERMAN

A car is useless in New York but necessary everywhere else. It's the same with good manners. **MIGNON MCLAUGHLIN**

In New York, tip the cab driver forty dollars if he doesn't mention his haemorrhoids. **DAVE BARRY**

Someone did a study of the three most often heard phrases in New York city. One is, 'Hey, taxi.' Two is, 'What train do I take to get to Bloomingdales.' And three is, 'Don't worry, it's just a flesh wound.'

DAVID LETTERMAN

A man robbed a bank in New York and got mugged on the way to the getaway car. **JACKIE MASON**

The difference between LA and New York drivers is that LA drivers tend to swerve all over the highway. New York drivers rarely have this problem. The body in the trunk makes a great stabiliser.

BROCK COHEN

I've just had cancer, brain surgery and a quadruple bypass. Thank God they still gave me my New York cabbie licence.   SID BRONSKI

The Captain was on the bridge, pretty sure he knew the way to New York but just to be on the safe side murmuring to himself, 'Turn right at Cherbourg, and then straight on.'   P.G. WODEHOUSE

'It's not the work I enjoy,' said the New York taxi-driver, 'it's the people I run into.'   STEVE MARTIN

New York is a city of seven million people so decadent that when I leave it I never dare look back lest I turn into salt and the bus conductor throw me over his left shoulder for good luck.

FRANK SULLIVAN

The astonishing thing about crossing New York from the airport to the heart of Broadway is that one isn't astonished.

SIMONE SIGNORET

London greets the stranger with a sleepy grunt. Paris giggles. New York howls.   P.G. WODEHOUSE

New York taxi drivers try to live up to the reputation all taxi drivers have, that of being wits. As I'm in the wit business myself, I object to competition.   BRENDAN BEHAN

The New York City police have now got cops on bicycles. It's a little embarrassing when you get arrested like this. You've got to ride all the way back to the police station on the handlebars.

DAVID LETTERMAN

Most people in New York don't have cars, so if you want to kill a person you have to take the subway.

GEORGE CARLIN

Jeremy Bentham thought that human beings had but two desires: gain and pleasure. He would have been at home in New York.

GORE VIDAL

The crime problem in New York is getting really serious. The other day the Statue of Liberty had both hands up.

JAY LENO

People say the dumbest things sometimes. 'Hey, man, you quit smoking – you'll get your sense of smell back.' I live in New York City. I've got news for you. I don't want my f****** sense of smell back.

BILL HICKS

New York isn't a city. It's a congerie of rotten villages.

JAMES M. CAIN

Fall in New York is so pretty, watching the trash change colours.

BILL CORONEL

New York's got humid. Your strength is gone. For the last two weeks New Yorkers have been giving each other only half a finger.

DAVID LETTERMAN

How many New Yorkers does it take to change a lightbulb?
One, you asshole!

AL PACINO

New York is the place where, if you have talent and you believe in yourself and you show people what you can do, then some day maybe – just maybe – you could get shoved in front of a moving train.

DAVE BARRY

There are two million interesting people in New York, and only seventy-eight in Los Angeles.

NEIL SIMON

New York now has 200 new portable toilets. They're yellow, have four wheels and a driver with a weird name.

JAY LENO

On my first day in New York a guy asked me if I knew where Central Park was. When I told him I didn't, he said, 'Do you mind if I mug you here then?'

PAUL MERTON

According to a recent poll, half of New Yorkers say they would never move out of the city. Mostly because their probation wouldn't allow it.

CONAN O'BRIEN

I come from New York where, if you fall down, someone will pick you up by your wallet.

AL MCGUIRE

New York is made out of modelling clay.

TRUMAN CAPOTE

When I first went to New York I was warned to look out for the pitfalls, and I did. But it was Sunday and they were all closed.

ROBERT BENCHLEY

New York is a narrow island off the coast of New Jersey devoted to the pursuit of lunch.

RAYMOND SOKOLOV

I've been a New Yorker for ten years and the only people who are nice to me turn out to be the Moonies.

P.J. O'ROURKE

New York is like living inside Stephen King's brain during an aneurism.

KEVIN ROONEY

Newspaper's too thick, lavatory paper too thin.

WINSTON CHURCHILL ASKED FOR HIS VIEWS ON
NEW YORK AFTER A VISIT THERE

New York is a place where you go to be lonely.

PAUL SCHRADER

OUT OF THIS WORLD

We've sent a man to the moon, which is 290,000 miles away. The centre of the earth is only 4,000 miles. You could drive there in a week. Why has nobody ever done it? **ANDY ROONEY**

A cartoon a few years ago showed a returning astronaut being interviewed by reporters. 'Is there life on Mars?' they asked him. 'Well,' he replied, 'there's a little on Saturday nights, but it's pretty dull the rest of the week.' **ADRIAN BERRY**

One small step for man … a taxi ride for Ronnie Corbett.

BARRY CRYER

It's time for the human race to enter the solar system. **DAN QUAYLE**

My ambition is to host a TV chat show with Neil Armstrong and never mention the moon. **ARDAL O'HANLON**

Space isn't remote at all. It's only an hour's drive away if your car could go straight upwards. **FRED HOYLE**

The drive towards complex technical achievement offers a clue to why the US is good at space gadgetry and bad at slum problems.

J.K. GALBRAITH

In the space age, man will be able to go around the world in two hours – one hour for flying and the other to get to the airport.

NEIL MCELROY

If the Irish Air Corps had a frequent flier programme, government ministers could probably get to the moon and back on their accumulated points.   JOHN BRUTON

I'd move to Los Angeles if Australia and New Zealand were swallowed by a tidal wave, if there was a bubonic plague in Europe and if Africa disappeared from some Martian attack.

RUSSELL CROWE

We don't need to leave earth to get a hostile alien environment. We already have Miami.   DAVE BARRY

China said it wants to start putting people into space. Not to explore – just to get rid of some of them.   JAY LENO

Houston – we've got a problem.   BOBBY BROWN, ATTRIB.

If half the engineering effort that went into research on the American bosom had gone into our guided missile programme, we would now be running hot dog stands on the moon.   AL CAPP

Rangers have been so far ahead in this game, now they've gone to, literally, another planet.   SOCCER COMMENTATOR ON
RADIO SCOTLAND

ROADHOGS

My son is a pretty good driver. Careful to signal his turns. That's what worries me. He'll be driving in Miami where nobody else, not even the police, does this. If Miami motorists were to see a turn signal there's no telling how they'd react. They could become alarmed and start shooting.
DAVE BARRY

One of the first things they teach you in Driver's Ed is where to put your hand on the steering wheel: at ten o'clock and two o'clock. I put mine at 9.45 and 2.15 to give myself an extra half hour to get where I'm going.
GEORGE CARLIN

The worst drivers are women in people carriers, men in white vans and people in baseball caps. That's just about everyone.

PAUL O'GRADY

When I drove home from the hospital after my baby was born it was the first time in my life I obeyed all the traffic laws. I had another life to take care of.

WILL SMITH

'One Lady Owner' on a car ad means 'batty old dame who used it only for short, cylinder-degrading, battery-wasting journeys, didn't know you had to put oil in it, and never quite mastered that funny little pedal on the left.'

RUSSELL ASH

He had his driving licence taken away for life in Ireland. This was quite a remarkable feat since the Highway Code is not the most zealously observed piece of legislation in Limerick. However, they couldn't overlook the fact that he had managed to drive his car into a corporation bus. Twice.

ELIZABETH HARRISON ON HER FIRST
HUSBAND RICHARD HARRIS

All you need for my kamikaze Death Squadron Rally are: Two or more competitors and vehicles, one copy of the Highway Code, and one blowtorch. How to Play: First burn your copy of the Highway Code. Rule 1: All road signs must be treated as if they gave exactly the opposite order. Rule 2: You must always drive at double the speed limit. The winner is the person who reaches the destination first, or the competitor with the least severe head injuries.

ADRIAN EDMONDSON

WHAT'S THE DAMAGE?

My garage's motto seems to be, 'If it ain't broke, we'll break it'.

JERRY SEINFELD

I don't know anything about automobile repairs. If you ask me to fix a car it's like asking Ray Charles to drive it. **ROBERT MURRAY**

Man's heart expands to tinker with his car
For this is Sunday morning, Fate's great bazaar. **LOUIS MACNEICE**

The garage mechanic lifted the bonnet. 'If I was you, sir,' he said, 'I'd keep the oil and change the car.' **GEORGE COOTE**

A man is at his most useful when changing a flat tyre.

RITA RUDNER

A garage charged me £100 to tow me off a motorway. I got my own back though. All the time he was towing I kept my brakes on.

LES DAWSON

The gas station attendant looked at the car and said, 'You got a flat tyre.' I said, 'No, the other three just swelled up.'   BILL ENGVALL

Auto Repair Service. Free pick-up and delivery. Try us once and you'll never go anywhere again.   GENUINE NEWSPAPER ADVERT

There are two types of car owners. The first type left school early. Such people crawl under cars, adjust the grommets, strip down the carburettor manifold, suck petrol through the sump gasket, spit it out manfully and make the car go. The other type is the educated few. We're strong on the ontological insecurity of nineteenth-century novelists. When our cars stop we ring the AA as soon as we have finished crying.   JOE BENNETT

At first glance you might think cars are just inanimate hunks of metal that are incapable of thinking. Get real. Most of them figure you're going to run their wheels off on the weekend so they just refuse to go. If it's winter, the electric windows will go down and freeze there. They know you have to go the distance to find a mechanic on duty.

ERMA BOMBECK

There's no damage to the car, except to the car itself.

MURRAY WALKER

ANIMAL WRITES

Take most people, they're crazy about cars. They worry if they get a little scratch on them, and they're always talking about how many miles they get to the gallon. I don't even like old cars. I'd rather have a goddam horse. A horse is at least human, for God's sake.

J.D. SALINGER

To give you an idea how fast we travelled, we left Spokane with two rabbits and when we got to Topeka, we still had only two.

BOB HOPE

Sheep really are pretty dumb. They're not even aware they're of great use for making woolly jumpers, or when they're dead making sheepskin coats for second-hand car dealers.

BONO

Paul Tracy has been in the grass so often the chipmunks know him by name.

PAUL PAGE

It is statistically proven
In chapter and in verse
That in a car-and-hedgehog fight
The hedgehog comes off worse.

PAM AYRES

They say animal behaviour can warn you when an earthquake is coming. The night before that last earthquake hit, our family dog took the car keys and drove to Arizona.

BOB HOPE

A Norwich Union customer collided with a cow. The questions and answers on the claim form were as follows:

Q   What warning was given by you?
A   Horn.
Q   What warning was given by the other party?
A   Moo.

Winning is everything. The only ones who remember when you came second are your wife and your dog.   DAMON HILL

The buffalo isn't as dangerous as everyone makes him out to be. Statistics prove that in the United States more Americans are killed in automobile accidents every year than by buffalos.   ART BUCHWALD

The rat was always my role model in the animal kingdom with its high intelligence and its instinct for survival.   NIKI LAUDA

What's the last thing that goes through a fly's head when he hits your windscreen? His arse.   JOE O'DONNELL

Second-hand car dealers, like cats, can sense when someone is afraid of them.   DENIS NORDEN

What most of us need is more horsepower and less exhaust.
HERBERT PROCHNOW

There's a good way to find out if your wife loves you more than your dog does. Put them both in the trunk of the car and leave them there for an hour. When you open it, see which of them is happiest to see you.
JOHN DAVIS

WEIRD OR WHAT?

A friend of mine has invented an electric car. It's very economical, You can get from London to Manchester for just £5. There's only one problem: the extension cord costs £2,000. **STEWART GREEN**

There's a pecking order for celebrities at after-show parties. One time both Prince and Madonna circled a block in their limos for twenty minutes because neither of them wanted to be the first to arrive.

BOY GEORGE

Does anybody get the concept behind summer vacations with your folks? We didn't get along together in a five-bedroomed house. Dad's idea was to put all of us in a car and drive through the desert at the hottest time of the year. Good call, Dad. **BILL HICKS**

Anthony Hopkins once told me he got into his car, drove 1,000 miles for no reason, turned the car round and then drove home again.

JAMES IVORY

In this posh new restaurant they have a menu with *Poulet a la Chevrolet* on it. That's a chicken that was run over by a truck.

HAL ROACH

Receptionists in doctors' offices are now there to protect the doctor. 'I'd like to see the doctor please'. 'Why?' 'Well I was hoping he'd help me change the tyres of the bloody car!' **DAVE ALLEN**

My next-door neighbour just had a pacemaker installed. They're still working the bugs out, though. Every time he makes love, my garage door opens. **BOB HOPE**

The craziest thing I ever did at Monte Carlo? Letting my wife go shopping. **MICHAEL ANDRETTI**

My chauffeur is a bit peculiar. He prefers to spend the weekend with his family than with me.

MICHAEL WINNER

As you get older you need to sleep more. My favourite time is on the motorway during rush hour.

BOB HOPE

I used to hate it when my father carried me on his shoulders. Especially when we were in the car.

ARDAL O'HANLON

I'm trying very hard to understand this generation. They've adjusted the timetable for childbearing so that the menopause and teaching a sixteen-year-old to drive a car will occur in the same week.

ERMA BOMBECK

I'm so addicted to cars I'm thinking of checking into the Henry Ford Clinic.

TIM TAYLOR

Ah Irishman's wife died and he was told he would be joined by his mother-in-law in the hearse that took the corpse to the graveyard. 'Very well,' he said reluctantly, 'but 'twill spoil the day for me.'

JIMMY O'DEA

The sport of skiing consists of wearing $300 worth of clothes and equipment and driving 200 miles in the snow in order to stand around a bar and get drunk.

P.J. O'ROURKE

I hate getting that smog check. Last week I bought a car and it failed inspection, which really sucks. Because the ozone layer is going, and soon we're going to need to breathe the smog my car creates.

JOEL WARSHAW

CASH FLOW

Big-money lottery winners have been found statistically to be no happier than those paralysed following a major car accident, six months after each event.

RAJ PERSAUD

Money differs from an automobile, a mistress or cancer in being equally important to those who have it and those who do not.

KENNETHY GALBRAITH

When my doctor told me he'd have me on my feet in two weeks he was right: I had to sell the car to pay the bill.

BERNARD MANNING

I make movies the same way I buy oil for my car. Every now and then I check the dipstick and if it's low I tank up. It's all about money.

MARLON BRANDO

Unless you decide to blow your brains out, drive your car over a cliff, lie down on some convenient stretch of railway line or shop extensively at the local chemist, there is no way in which you can deprive yourself of the pastime of worrying about money.

ROBERT MORLEY

Very often a gentleman's wife will have her own car, particularly if she can afford to buy it herself. Anything that is small and uncomfortable will do.

DOUGLAS SUTHERLAND

I like cheap airlines as much as the next man but I draw the line at having to bring my own parachute.

BOB MONKHOUSE

If you travel as much as we do you appreciate how much more comfortable aircraft have become, unless you travel in economy class, which sounds ghastly.

PRINCE PHILIP

I saw a truck today. On the side of the door it said, 'Driver Has No Cash'. I'm broke too, but I don't plaster it all over the side of my car.

MARGARET SMITH

Nowadays they spend £10,000 for a school bus to pick the kids up right at their doors so they don't have to walk. Then they spend £20,000 for a gym so they can get some exercise.

RED BLANCHARD

What Englishman will give his mind to politics as long as he can afford to keep a motor car?

GEORGE BERNARD SHAW

Anybody who has to ask what is the upkeep of a yacht cannot afford one.

J.P. MORGAN

Look at all the buses that want exact change. I figure if I give them exact change they should take me exactly where I want to go.

GEORGE WALLACE

Passenger to chauffeur: Do you stop at the Ritz?
Chauffeur: On the salary I earn? You must be joking.

ANDREW MIDDLETON

I only go to Las Vegas for sentimental reasons – to visit my money.

FRANK SINATRA

People don't want a cheaper car. They want an expensive car that costs less.

JACKIE MASON

SHANKING IT

Pedestrian: Anyone who is knocked down by a motor car.

J.B. MORTON

The Evening Herald says a man is knocked down by a car every three hours. He must be getting fed up of it.

SHAUN CONNORS

Pedestrians should not cross the road at traffic lights until the little green man appears. They can then cross in perfect safety, provided they can cover 22 feet in three seconds.

LAMBERT JEFFRIES

Pedestrian: Excuse me, officer, could you tell me the quickest way to the hospital?

Policeman: Yes, just stay where you are in the middle of the road.

EUGENE MISTED

Did you hear about the driver who knocked a pedestrian 8 feet in the air and then sued him for leaving the scene of the accident?

FRED PERRY

Restore human legs as a means of travel. Pedestrians rely on food for fuel and need no special parking facilities.

LEWIS MUMFORD

Last year on Father's Day my son gave me something I've always wanted – the keys to my car.

AL STERLING

Anyone who walks in Beverly Hills is a celebrity.

GROUCHO MARX

DRIVING MISS DAISY

There are only three ages for women in Hollywood – Babe, District Attorney, and Driving Miss Daisy.
GOLDIE HAWN

They say the car a man drives is an extension of his penis. Is that why so many men drive small, fast cars?
JENNIFER VALLY

People accuse me of being a 'Love 'em and leave 'em' type but that's not true. I let them catch me out and then they leave me.
EDDIE IRVINE

A quick grope by the gate or in the back seat of a car was as far as I ever went in sexual terms in my youth. In those days I still believed you might get pregnant through your knickers.
GLORIA HUNNIFORD

Her nostrils are so big, when you kiss her it's like driving into a two-car garage.
HAL ROACH

Love is the hum that means the heart's stalled motor has begun working again.
VLADIMIR MAYAKOVSKY

You have to treat a car like a woman. You have to coax it sometimes to get the best out of it, you have to correct it, and at times, maybe on a difficult circuit, you have to give it a really good thrashing, because that is the only way it understands.
JACKIE STEWART

A girl should hang on to her youth, but not while he's driving.
SEAMUS O'LEARY

The funny thing about girls is that they always think they can change you and that in the end you'll come round, declare undying love and settle down in a cottage with a couple of kids.
EDDIE IRVINE

The two great problems in life: How to get a car going in the morning, and a woman going at night.

ROY 'CHUBBY' BROWN

Cornering is like bringing a woman to climax.

JACKIE STEWART

Playboy never wants you to think the pictures are posed: 'We just happened to catch Kathy typing nude on top of a Volvo this morning.'

ELAYNE BOOSLER

I was once asked what I'd do if a bird crapped on my windscreen. I replied, 'I wouldn't ask her out again.'

JIM DAVIDSON

There are proven psychological techniques for dealing with conflict in your marriage. For example, on long car trips, one of you should ride in the trunk.

DAVE BARRY

He told me it was his first date but he was still able to change gear with his knees while he was kissing me.

WENDY DENNIS

I was dating a stunt man for a while. It's a lot like dating regular guys really. He picks me up, takes me out to dinner and so on. But when he drops me off he doesn't stop the car.

JENNIFER SIEGEL

Men consider driving back to her place as part of the foreplay.

MATT GROENING

According to *Men's Health* magazine, the average man has had sex in a car fifteen times. That's something to keep in mind the next time you're looking for a used car.

JAY LENO

In our family the rule was: Never keep a soda can between your legs when you're in the car. My father told me a story about a man who did that and got into a bad car wreck. And, bang, he lost his Johnson.

BRAD PITT

With a Corrado, as with all other performance cars, only three things matter: How much does it cost? How fast does it go? Can I pull birds in it?

JEREMY CLARKSON

The fake tan is a marvellous invention. While everyone else is on the beach trying to go brown, you're in the hotel shagging a waiter.

JENNY ECLAIR

THE KNACKER'S YARD

My life is passing in front of my eyes. The worst part is, I'm driving a used car.
WOODY ALLEN

Compromise is the secret of a happy marriage. My next-door neighbour wanted a second-hand car and his wife wanted a fur coat. They couldn't afford both so they compromised. She got the coat but they keep it in the garage.
LES DAWSON

Used cars aren't all they're jacked up to be.
GRAFFITI

The plane was so old, when we stopped to re-fuel we took on wood.
FRED ALLEN

The Texan was boasting about the size of his ranch, 'I get into my car at 6 a.m. every day, and by nightfall I still haven't finished driving round it' he told his farmhand. The farmhand replied, 'I used to have a car like that once, but I got rid of it!'
MICHAEL HARKNESS

Good agents are like good second-hand car salesmen. They have to be good liars.   ROY 'CHUBBY' BROWN

I'm doing what I can to help the environment: I started a compost pile. It's in the back seat of my car.   JANINE DITULLIO

The starter went wrong, and after a week or two I also lost the starting-handle, so the only possible way to start the car was to put her in gear, give her a push, and when the motor started, jump in and drive away. At the beginning it happened occasionally that the car ran faster than I did.   GEORGE MIKES

After I'd switched off the ignition the whole inside of the bonnet would go on shaking for about three minutes, like a dog coming out of the water.   DENIS NORDEN

Q. How do you use the airbags on a Lada?
A. If you're in an accident, start blowing.   INTERNET JOKE

ASHES TO ASHES
(The Iceland Volcano)

The volcanic ash from Iceland disrupted air travel all over Europe. Everything's grounded – commercial flights, private jets and so on. The only things still flying are Toyotas.

JAY LENO

I woke up this morning to find every surface in the house covered in a layer of dust and a foul stench of sulphur in the air. No change there, then: I've been married to the bone-idle slob for twenty years.

E-FORWARDS.COM

Call it Iceland's revenge, but there's no more effective way for a small country to get its own back on a larger one than to have an erupting volcano in its midst. No trade embargo, however effective, could compete.

JEREMY WARNER

I see that America has declared war on Iceland. Apparently they're accusing them of harbouring a weapon of mass disruption.

ANDRE, TWITTER

What did the aeroplane say to the volcano? 'Shut up, you ash-hole'.

JOHN, TWITTER

BBC News said we all face prolonged air chaos as a result of the volcanic ash. How can there be air chaos when we're all stuck on the ground?

E-FORWARDS.COM

According to Sky News the emergency services were afraid they could be swamped by a torrent of melted ice. I believe the technical term for this is 'water'.

E-FORWARDS.COM

Apparently this is a communication problem. The message from money-strapped Europe had a letter missing. It should have read, 'Send Us Your CASH'.

LOUISE PARK-AHONEN

First Iceland goes bankrupt. After that it sets itself on fire. This has insurance scam written all over it.

JOHN, TWITTER

Experts have warned that it could take years of work by experienced professionals to clean up after the volcano. That's why Mum's gone to Iceland.

E-FORWARDS.COM

I travelled to Iceland by car ferry last week. When I arrived the Sat Nav said, 'You have now reached your dusty nation'.　　JOHN, TWITTER

Nobody teaches volcanoes to erupt any more than nobody teaches you how to choose a wife. Natural disasters just happen.

BRENDAN GRACE

I nearly blew my top when I heard about the Iceland volcano. There were a lot of people spewing false information, and many were just full of hot air.　　JOHN, TWITTER

FA Cup Final Prediction: Ash-ley Coal scores the winner against Pompeii.

E-FORWARDS.COM

There's no volcano in Iceland. Chuck Norris is just having a barbecue.

JOHN, TWITTER

I see that all UK flights are grounded for the second day in a row. They must have strict parents!

E-FORWARDS.COM

It's a bit early for Iceland volcano jokes. We should wait a while for the dust to settle.

SOL, TWITTER

BETTER SAFE THAN SORRY

Drive carefully. The life you save may be … mine.   JAMES DEAN

I don't think my wife likes me very much. When I had a heart attack she *wrote* for an ambulance.   FRANK CARSON

In order to cut down on in-flight fatalities, American Airlines has decided to upgrade the medical kits on all its planes. Each kit will now contain common lifesaving drugs, a heart defibrillator, and a spare plane.

NORM MACDONALD

Bullfighters probably don't bother with seatbelts.   RITA RUDNER

Car owners of the world unite. You have nothing to lose but your manners, and someone else's life.   COLIN MACINNES

I'm strapping myself into the seat in case I fall out if the plane comes to a sudden stop. Like against a mountain.   SHELLEY BERMAN

I don't trust trains. I remember those old movies where halfway through the journey somebody would reach up above the window and yank down on the brake cord. I don't want to be on any form of mass transit where the general public has access to brakes. I'd hate to find out that we went off the tracks at 200mph because Gus thought he saw a woodchuck.   DENNIS MILLER

The only country with a better air safety record than the US is the Republic of Kyrgyzstan, which has only one plane and can't figure out how to start it.   DAVE BARRY

Airline hostesses show you how to use a seatbelt in case you haven't been in a car since 1965. **JERRY SEINFELD**

It was a pretty little plane rather like a cottage – all blue and white with plush curtains. No nonsense about fastening your safety belt. And no safety belt. **NANCY MITFORD**

Who are safer drivers, men or women? According to a new survey, 55 per cent of adults feel women are most responsible for fender-benders, while 78 per cent blame men for most fatal crashes. Please note that the percentages do not add up to 100 per cent because the math was done by a woman. **NORM MACDONALD**

My big fear is driving behind a truck with those big iron rebars. If it stops the bar goes right through my forehead. It doesn't kill me but they can't remove it so I have to accessorise it. **CARRIE SNOW**

JOYS OF YOUTH

I much prefer travelling in non-British ships. There's none of that nonsense about women and children first. **SOMERSET MAUGHAM**

We've been having some trouble with the school bus. It keeps bringing the kids back. **BRUCE LANSKY**

Try flying any plane with a baby if you want a sense of what it must have been like to be a leper in the fourteenth century.

NORA EPHRON

I know some people are against drunk driving but sometimes you've just got no choice. Those kids gotta get to school. **DAVE ATELL**

When I was a teenager, every Saturday night I'd ask my father for the car keys and he'd always say the same thing: 'All right, son, but don't lose them because some day we may get a car.'

YAKOV SMIRNOFF

Foreign travel broadens the minds of the young – and the hips of the middle-aged. **SPIKE HUGHES**

The problem with a 'Baby on Board' sign is that parents don't take it down when the baby isn't on board. They should have a sign saying 'Baby at Auntie Jean's'. That way we could adjust our driving.

ARTHUR SMITH

My children are at the perfect age – too old to cry at night and too young to borrow my car. **MAURICE SILVER**

Never lend your car to anyone to whom you've given birth.

ERMA BOMBECK

The bus conductor didn't believe me when I said I was young enough to qualify for half fare. 'Can I help it if I worry?' I asked.

JAMES MITCHELL LEAR

When I'm driving I see a sign that says, 'Caution: Small Children Playing'. I slow down, but then it occurs to me: I'm not afraid of small children.

JONATHAN KATZ

The best way to keep your children at home is to make the atmosphere pleasant. And let the air out of their tyres.

DOROTHY PARKER

Who needs Disney World? My kids get just as much of a thrill when we drive the car through the car wash.

OLIVER COE

Boys drive small cars incredibly fast on suburban streets in order to meet girls and impress them. Men drive big cars incredibly fast on motorways in order to meet finance directors and impress them. Boys love their cars. Men love their no-claims bonus.

GUY BROWNING

Can you abandon a child along a public highway for kicking Daddy's seat for 600 miles?

ERMA BOMBECK

A child on a farm sees a plane fly overhead and dreams of a faraway place. A traveller on the plane sees the farmhouse and dreams of home.   CARL BURNS

Never play peek-a-boo with a child on a long plane trip. There's no end to the game. You finally have to grab him by the bib and shout, 'Look, it's always going to be me'.   RITA RUDNER

Trying to bring up children today is a bit like hanging onto an aircraft as it's taking off.   GABRIEL BYRNE

Never have more children than you have car windows.

ERMA BOMBECK

LEARNER PERMITS

Do driving instructors all have to imitate a Dalek when they speak? 'Please. Turn. Left. At. The. Next. Available. Turning.' **MARY KENNY**

My mom taught me how to drive. I can't drive worth a damn but I can change all my clothes at a Stop light. **CRAIG SHOEMAKER**

There are few things in life more satisfying than having your son teach you how to play tennis, unless it is having a semi-truck run over your foot. **ERMA BOMBECK**

Kermit: Fozzie, where did you learn to drive?
Fozzie: I took a correspondence course. **JERRY JUHL**

My wife had her driver's test the other day. She got 8 out of 10. The other 2 guys jumped clear. RODNEY DANGERFIELD

It didn't take me long to learn to drive, just about four cars.

JOEY BISHOP

Real Answers to Driving School Questions:
Q. Do you yield when a blind pedestrian is crossing the road?
A. What for? He can't see my licence plate.
Q. What is the difference between a flashing red traffic light and a flashing yellow traffic light?
A. The colour. E-TALES

I've never seen an ad for post office van drivers but I suspect they insist on some Grand Prix experience. Either that or they trawl the schizophrenic wards of psychiatric hospitals. JEREMY CLARKSON

The main curse of life is that when you're learning golf you hit nothing and when you're learning motoring you hit everything.

DUBLIN OPINION

WARNING SIGNALS

If you ever see me in a queue at the railway booking office, join the other one. Because there'll be a chap in front of me who's trying to send a rhinoceros to Tokyo.

BASIL BOOTHROYD

The problem with the designated driver programme is that it's not a desirable job. If you ever get suckered into it, have fun with it. At the end of the night drop everyone off at the wrong house.

JEFF FOXWORTHY

You can sometimes bring reluctant sneezes on by staring into lights. Don't do this when you're driving. You may get a powerful and satisfying sneeze but it will be your last one.

GUY BROWNING

The secret of driving in London is never to catch any other driver's eye. Whatever you do, never look at him when one of you has to give way – especially if he's a cab driver. Pretend you're dead ignorant, then they have to give way. Take a dead stupid nit of a woman driver, crossing one way and with her blinker going the other – they all get out of the way.   **BILL NAUGHTON**

As you exit the plane, be sure to gather all of your belongings. Anything left behind will be distributed evenly among the flight attendants. Please do not leave children or spouses.   **EMAIL JOKE**

The only way to be sure of catching a train is to miss the one before it.   **G.K. CHESTERTON**

When you're behind cell phone drivers it's generally wise to wait patiently for a few moments until they ram into a bridge abutment. Then you can pass safely on whatever side has the least amount of flame spewing out.   **DAVE BARRY**

TERMINAL ILLNESS

I did not fully understand the term 'terminal illness' until I saw Heathrow for myself.
DENNIS POTTER

Airplane travel is nature's way of making you look like your passport photo.
AL GORE

It can hardly be a coincidence that no language on earth has ever produced the expression 'as pretty as an airport.'
DOUGLAS ADAMS

Doc Daneeka hated to fly. He felt imprisoned in an airplane. In an airplane there was absolutely no place in the world to go except to another part of the airplane.
JOSEPH HELLER

Travelling by air is demoralising. You are treated like a gentleman.
KINGSLEY MARTIN

Nothing is as uninteresting as looking at clouds from the inside.
RICHARD GORDON

There are two reasons to sit in the back of an airplane. Either you have diarrhoea or you're anxious to meet people who do.
HENRY KISSINGER

The Americans cannot build aeroplanes. They are better at making refrigerators and razor blades.
HERMANN GOERING TO HITLER IN 1940: HIS JUDGMENT WAS SOMEWHAT OFF, AS HE WAS TO DISCOVER THE FOLLOWING YEAR AFTER THE INVASION OF PEARL HARBOUR

Dublin Airport is an A&E ward for slightly healthier people.
DAVID MCWILLIAMS

James Hunt once made the tabloids for inadvertently peeing on Esther Rantzen during a flight from Australia, having found all the aircraft's toilets in use.   RICHARD WILLIAMS

We're now approaching Belfast Airport. Please fasten your seat-belts, extinguish your cigarettes and put your watches back 300 years.

NIALL TOIBIN

I feel about airplanes the way I feel about diets. It seems to me that they're wonderful things for other people to go on.   JEAN KERR

There's nothing like an airport for bringing you down to earth.

RICHARD GORDON

I wouldn't mind dying for France, but not for Air France.

CHARLES DE GAULLE AFTER A ROCKY FLIGHT, ATTRIB.

I'll take three hours in the dentist's waiting room with four cavities and an impacted wisdom tooth in preference to fifteen minutes at any airport waiting for an aeroplane.   PATRICK CAMPBELL

I think I embarrassed the lady next to me on the plane. I was on one of those flights that you sleep on … and I sleep in the nude.

JOHNNY DARK

The only places they show my movies now is on airplanes. Nobody can leave the cinema.   BURT REYNOLDS

Murphy threw up on the plane and the air hostess was outraged. 'There's a bag in front of you,' she said, 'Why didn't you use that?' 'I don't even know the woman,' Murphy replied.   CONAL GALLEN

Cork's airport has some unusual features, including typhoon gusts from the North Atlantic that toss arriving planes around like confetti, and tractors that are kept on call to plough lakes of torrential rain off its runways.   DAVID MONAGHAN

My biological clock is ticking so loud, they search me going into planes.   MARIAN KEYES

MOTOR ACCESSORIES

My wife and I have decked out our bed like the back seat of the car where we first dated. We're trying to make out like we used to.

BUD HEWSON

My kids wanted a DVD fitted in the headrest of the car. I was against this but my wife went ahead and fitted one without telling me. To get my own back I recorded a three-hour film of the back of my head.

JACK DEE

All cars should have phones in them and their licence plates should be their phone number so you can call them up and tell them to get the hell out of the way.

JOHN MENDOZA

I don't like the idea that people can call you in your car. I think there's news you shouldn't get at 60mph. 'Pregnant? Whoah!' But if we're gonna have car phones I think we should have car answering machines: 'Tom's at home right now, but as soon as he goes out he'll get back to you.'

TOM PARKS

He had a two-way stereo system in his car for years: his wife in the front and her mother in the back.

BOB MONKHOUSE

Hood ornaments were lovely and gave a sense of respect. They took them away because, 'If you can save one human life' – that's always the argument - 'It's worth it.' Actually I'd be willing to trade a dozen human lives for a nice hood ornament.

MICHAEL O'DONOGHUE

When I press the brake pedal the headlights go on, and a voice speaks from the steering wheel.

SPIKE MILLIGAN

My mother has this car with a computer. It talks like a Jewish car: 'Eh, why even go? It's windy out.'

RICHARD LEWIS

Motor cars have never been quite the same for me since people stopped winding them up at the front with a handle.

ARTHUR MARSHALL

Many business people use mobile phones in their cars. Of course this is strictly forbidden unless you have a hands-free set. Men tend to ignore this rule because they're used to driving virtually hands free anyway while they excavate the inner recesses of their nostrils with one hand and fiddle with their genitals with the other.

GUY BROWNING

If the automobile had followed the same development cycle as the computer, a Rolls Royce today would cost $100, get a million miles per gallon, and explode once a year, killing everyone inside.

ROBERT CRINGELY

IMMUTABLE LAWS OF TRAVELLING

If there's only room for five on the bus, you'll be sixth in the queue.

LEONARD ROSSITER

The car of tomorrow is being driven on the highway of yesterday by the driver of today.

ROLFE ARROW

Rowe's Rule: The odds are five to six that the light at the other end of the tunnel is the headlight of the oncoming train.

PAUL DICKSON

Slip the edge of your offside tyre over a continuous white line in an empty lane at four o'clock in the morning and a squad car immediately pops out of the long grass.

PATRICK CAMPBELL

The quickest way to make a red light turn green is to try and find something in the glove compartment.

BILLY CONNOLLY

An old car that's going well will continue to do so until you fit it with four new tyres.

LEONARD ROSSITER

Removing the faults in a stagecoach may produce a perfect stagecoach, but it is unlikely to produce the first motor car.

EDWARD DE BONO

You're either on the bus or off the bus. If you're on it and you get left behind then you'll find it again. If you're off the bus in the first place then it won't matter a damn.

KEN KESEY

When the weight of the paperwork equals the weight of the plane, the plane will fly.

DONALD DOUGLAS

General Laws of Air Travel:

1. Your departure gate will always be the farthest from the terminal, regardless of number.
2. The plane will not shake until the meal is served.
3. The amount of turbulence will be in direct proportion to the heat of your coffee.
4. The person next to you will either be a white knuckler or will have need for the little white bag.
5. When you finally get to the lavatory, the 'Return to Your Seat' will go on.

HAL ROACH

One leak will sink a ship, and one sin will destroy a sinner.

JOHN BUNYAN

Airplane turbulence is one of the best laxatives known to mankind.

JASPAR CARROTT

FOOD FOR THOUGHT

Stay humble. Always answer the phone no matter who else is in the car.
JACK LEMMON

In the history of the world, no one has ever washed a rented car.
LARRY SUMMERS

Wooler in Northumberland is marketed as the gateway to the Cheviots. It should more properly be called the arsehole of the Cheviots. I'm sure that would attract more tourists.
CHRIS DONALD

I was in Margate last year for the summer season. A friend of mine said it was good for rheumatism. So I went there and got it.
TOMMY COOPER

Every driver in Birmingham looks like a forced rhubarb.
JEREMY CLARKSON

Positioning is vital for sunbathing. For a start you need to be in the sun, so anywhere outside the UK is good.   **GUY BROWNING**

Old age is like waiting in the departure lounge of life. Fortunately, I live in England so the train is bound to be late.   **MILTON SHULMAN**

Of all noxious animals, the most noxious is a tourist. And of all tourists, the most vulgar, ill-bred, offensive and loathsome is the British tourist.
REVD FRANCIS KILVERT

Frinton-on-Sea is so dull it carries a Government Health Warning. It caused hilarity by issuing a tourist brochure.   **GEOFFREY ATKINSON**

The English always have their wars in someone else's country.
BRENDAN BEHAN

EGO TRIPPERS

In one year I travelled 450,000 miles by air. That's 18½ times around the world – or once round Howard Cosell's head.　　**JACKIE STEWART**

He was the sort of fellow who would insist on being seated in the No Smoking compartment of the lifeboat.　　**JOHN PEPPER**

The Australian's loving relationship with his car has become commonplace. He fondles each nut and bolt in interminable conversations in the pub. He strips it, lays it on the lawn and greases its nipples while his wife wonders whether he will ever better his indoor average of one-a-month.

IAN MOFFIT

When a man confronts catastrophe on the road he looks in his purse. But a woman looks in her mirror.　　**MARGARET TURNBULL**

You suddenly realise you're no longer in government when you get into the back of your car and it doesn't go anywhere.

MALCOLM RIFKIND

People on ego trips should do others a favour and buy one-way tickets.

HAL ROACH

Men drive fast, we're told, because the car is an extension of the penis. But if it were, surely they'd just back in and out of the garage. Or maybe just polish it all the time.

JEREMY HARDY

He would write love letters to me from all over the world. Well, not actually love letters. They were more technical reports on his car.

TAORMINA RICH ON JAMES HUNT

EASY RIDERS

Male menopause is a lot more fun than female menopause. With female menopause you gain weight and get hot flashes. With male menopause you get to date young girls and drive motorcycles.

RITA RUDNER

A cousin of mine who was a Casualty surgeon in Manhattan tells me he and his colleagues had a one-word nickname for bikers: Donors.

STEPHEN FRY

The art of negotiation is learned from an early age. You'd be amazed how many teenagers get a car by asking for a motorcycle.

JAMES VARLEY

If You Can Read This, The Bitch Fell Off.

MOTORCYCLE JACKET SLOGAN

Motorcyclists who don't wear helmets should have their heads examined ... and they usually do,

FRED METCALF

I've always said that if a boy comes to take my daughters out on a motorbike I shall drop a match in the petrol tank.

JEREMY CLARKSON

The advantage of the rain is that, if you have a quick bike, there's no advantage.

BARRY SHEENE

GET LOST!

Getting on a plane I told the ticket lady, 'Send one of my bags to New York, one to Los Angeles and one to Miami.' She said, 'We can't do that.' I told her, 'You did last week!'   **BENNY YOUNGMAN**

Seasoned couple at the airlines reservations counter: 'Two tickets to wherever our luggage is going, please.'   **GEORGE COOTE**

Miami doesn't have a visitor-friendly airport. A cramped and dingy labyrinth, the message is clear: Just Try To Find Our Baggage Claim Area.   **DAVE BARRY**

Did you ever notice that the first piece of luggage on the carousel never belongs to anyone?   **ERMA BOMBECK**

I travel a lot. I've been to almost as many places as my luggage.   **BOB HOPE**

When my husband and I go on trips I get two jobs in the car. I get to read the map and also to ask directions when we get lost.   **RITA RUDNER**

TAKE A HIKE

Whenever I pick up a hitch-hiker I say, 'Put your seatbelt on. I want to try something I saw in a cartoon.'
STEVEN WRIGHT

Most men who hitch-hike have never sat in first class on an airplane.
RITA RUDNER

I was getting into my car and this bloke says to me, 'Can you give me a lift?' I said, 'Sure, you look great. The world's your oyster. Go for it.'
TOMMY COOPER

My doctor told me to get more exercise and fresh air. I told him I'd drive with the car window open.
ANGUS WALKER

TERROR-STRICKEN

I once dated a kamikaze pilot. He was really bad at it, though. He kept landing.

WENDY LIEBMAN

What do female kamikaze pilots say to their boyfriends on date nights? 'Does my bomb look big in this?'

INTERNET JOKE

It would be nice if the United States could bomb someone every day.

TED TURNER AFTER HEARING HIS CNN RATINGS WENT UP
DURING A MILITARY NEWS BROADCAST

An airplane full of lawyers was hijacked by terrorists. They promised to release one every hour unless their demands were met.

DENIS LEARY

Suicide bombers are promised 72 virgins. One would have done me.

ARDAL O'HANLON

Soon the only people flying to Europe will be terrorists. It will be, 'Armed or unarmed section please, sir?'

ROBIN WILLIAMS

The Americans don't really understand what's going on in Bosnia. To them it's the unspellables killing the unpronounceables.

P.J. ROURKE

DIRECTING TRAFFIC

An American tourist stopped in a village and said to a young boy, 'Can you tell me where this road goes to?' The boy said, 'It doesn't go nowhere. It stays right where it is.' HAL ROACH

Never ask for directions in Wales or you'll be washing spit out of your hair for a fortnight. ROWAN ATKINSON

An obstetrician once made the observation that male babies take longer to deliver. This bears out the theory I have long held that, even at birth, men are reluctant to ask directions anywhere.

ERMA BOMBECK

The likelihood of getting lost is directly proportional to the number of times the direction-giver says, 'You can't miss it.' HAL ROACH

Never ask an English person for directions. They're too polite to tell you if they don't know the way and will send you somewhere else instead – usually Wales. JOE O'CONNOR

RUNNING ON EMPTY

The only reason I was driving so fast was because I was trying to get home before the petrol ran out.

DUSTY YOUNG

Save Petrol. Make roads shorter.

GRAFFITI

Gas prices are so high in Chicago that cab drivers are taking the real way to the airport.

JAY LENO

A pedestrian is someone who thought he'd put petrol in his tank.

SAM LEVINSON

Gas is so expensive these days, guys are dating Monica Lewinsky for her siphoning skills.

JAY LENO

I went up to the petrol attendant. '£10, please,' I said. He was a nice guy. He handed me a tenner.

SIMON APPLETON

The reason the Spanish Armada sank was because it didn't get enough miles to the galleon.

GRAFFITI

Last Petrol Station Until The Next One.

SIGN SPOTTED IN RURAL ENGLAND

Three trains, cancelled to save fuel, are still running. But to show that they're officially cancelled, no passengers are allowed to travel on them.

DAILY WORKER

They're talking about making fuel from horse manure now, one thing's for sure – it will put a stop to siphoning.

BILLIE HOLIDAY

LOOK BACK IN ANGER

One of the delights of being a senior citizen is that it's easy to annoy young people. Step 1: Get in the car. Step 2: Turn the indicator. Step 3: Leave it on for 50 miles.　　　　**DAVID LETTERMAN**

Some guy hit my fender the other day. I said to him, 'Be fruitful and multiply.' But not in those words.　　　　**WOODY ALLEN**

Falling asleep at the wheel is one of the main causes of accidents today. You can avoid it by rolling down the window and screaming. Actually I do this anyway even when I'm not tired.　　　　**KEITH WALDEN**

Colin Farrell's TV interviews have more beeps than the M50 at rush hour.　　　　**ANITA MULLAN**

A fruit cart will always be overturned during the car chase in a movie, and an angry peddler will run into the middle of the street to shake his fist at the hero's departing vehicle.　　　　**ROGER EBERT**

There is no class of person more moved by hate than the motorist.
　　　　C.R. HEWITT

If you make a left turn from a right-hand lane you're probably just careless, and not at all what the driver behind called you.
　　　　HAL ROACH

Men swear more when they're in a car. Outside the car my husband is a perfect gentleman. Inside it he's a sailor with Tourette's Syndrome.
　　　　RITA RUDNER

A lot of people who fly into a rage make a bad landing. **WILL ROGERS**

Those signs that say 'Baby on Board' just make you want to hit the car harder. **SUE KOLINSKY**

A car phone is the ideal gift for a sadistic boss who tends to lose control when he shouts into the receiver. **RICK BAYAN**

If you ever want to torture my dad, tie him up and right in front of him, refold a road map incorrectly. **CATHY LADMAN**

The first thing I'm going to buy when I win the lottery is breast implants for my steering wheel. It will make rush hour much less stressful.

DOBIE MAXWELL

You know you're an aggressive driver when your horn is broken and you feel like your middle finger's been cut off. **DOUG GRAHAM**

I wonder what language truck drivers are using now that everyone else is using theirs? **BERYL PFIZER**

When my husband and I are in the car I usually let him drive. Because when I drive, he has a tendency to bite the dashboard.

RITA RUDNER

Footballers tend not to notice what's around them. I remember once on a tour of Italy the coach passed the Leaning Tower of Pisa. I pointed it out, only to be told, 'Shut up and deal!' **BOBBY CHARLTON**

OILED FOOLS

Don't drink and drive. Leave it on the dashboard.   **BRENDAN GRACE**

A beautiful blonde once drove me to drink. It's the only good thing she did.   **W.C. FIELDS**

A guard pulled me over and told me I was doing 80mph. I said I was only doing 60. He said 80. I said 60. Then my wife reached over and said to him, 'Guard, you'll never win an argument with my husband when he's drunk.'   **NOEL V. GINNITY**

My life so far has been the equivalent of driving a car at 140mph after ten pints.   **COLIN FARRELL**

The driver is safe then the roads are dry and the roads are safe when the driver is dry.   **CONOR FAUGHNAN**

I've decided to stop driving drunk. I can never remember where I've parked the bloody car.   **DAVE ALLEN**

My friends felt I was drinking too heavily and encouraged me to join the AA. Best thing I ever did. They're always there to give me a start if I get stuck in the pub car park.   BOB MONKHOUSE

I never drink when I fly.   CHRISTOPHER REEVE IN *SUPERMAN*

After I quit drinking I realised I'm the same asshole I always was. I just have fewer dents in my car.   ROBIN WILLIAMS

The air hostess offered me a glass of brandy, which I declined. Apparently I could get plastered drunk and become a nuisance, or I could pop pills or shoot heroin, but I wasn't allowed to smoke.
FR MICHAEL CLEARY AFTER BEING ON A
FLIGHT FROM DUBLIN TO LONDON

They say 40 per cent of accidents are drink-related. That means 60 per cent aren't. So what's the problem with my boozing?
DEAN MARTIN

Researchers at Colorado University say wine helps people lose weight. It's not the wine that causes the weight loss directly it's all the walking around you do trying to find your car.   JAY LENO

Bars are installing Breathalyser vending machines telling people whether they've had too much to drink. Apparently if you're drunk the machine warns you not to drive, and if you're really drunk it warns you not to call your ex-girlfriend.   CONAN O'BRIEN

Barbara Castle brought in seatbelts and drink-driving.
JOHN PRESCOTT

BROADENING THE ASS

Travel broadens the ass, not the mind.   ERNEST HEMINGWAY

A critic is a man who knows the way but can't drive the car.
                                                          KENNETH TYNAN

A tourist is a person who changes his car oil every four days and his
shirt once a week.   HERBERT PROCHNOW

I'm very emotional. I cry every time the lights go red.   RIK MAYALL

I don't like escalators. After the first hesitant step and the sensation of
the ground rising under one, I worry about an abrupt power failure or,
supposing myself to be wearing sandals, whether it is possible for the
sole to be caught in the final tread and whether I could face life with an
artificial foot.   ROBERT MORLEY

Some motorists almost live in their motor cars. It gratifies me to state
that these motorists generally die in their motor cars too.
                                                          G.K. CHESTERTON

On my last vacation it was raining day and night until I found out I was
sleeping in a carwash.   LEOPOLD FECHTNER

It's easier to find a travelling companion than to get rid of one.
                                                          ART BUCHWALD

Playing golf can be interesting, but not the part where you try to hit the
little ball: only the part where you drive the cart.
                                                          DAVE BARRY

I'd rather wake up in the middle of nowhere than in any city on earth.
                                                          STEVE McQUEEN

My mother is a travel agent for all guilt trips.   RUBY WAX

P.J. O'Rourke once described a pick-up truck as a back porch with an engine. This is unfair – to back porches.   JEREMY CLARKSON

People ask me if I missed rock 'n' roll when I was in the army. How could I? I was in tanks. That's all they do!   ELVIS PRESLEY

The heart and soul of any city is its whorehouses.   ERROL FLYNN

Frustrate a Frenchman and he will drink himself to death. Frustrate an Irishman and he will die of hypertension. A Dane will shoot himself while an American will get drunk, shoot *you*, and then establish a million-dollar aid programme for your relatives.   STUART RUDIN

While armchair travellers dream of going places, travelling armchairs dream of staying put.   ANNE TYLER

Britain's slow pace, its minimum risk policies and its mild climate make it the natural setting for losers.   QUENTIN CRISP

If you must give your child lessons, send him to driving school. He's much more likely to end up owning a Datsun than a Stradivarius.   FRAN LEBOWITZ

You know the best thing about gangs? They carpool.   JOHN MENDOZA

Travel is the most private of pleasures. There is no greater bore than the travel bore. We do not in the least want to hear what he has seen in Hong Kong.   VITA SACKVILLE-WEST

Nowadays you catch foreign travel rather as you caught influenza in the twenties.   GEORGE MIKES

Travel is 90 per cent anticipation and 10 per cent recollection.
                                   EDWARD STREETER

The British tourist is always happy abroad so long as the natives are waiters.   ROBERT MORLEY

Every year one reads of motorised parties leaving London for the Far East. Some, with steaming radiators or lack of funds, get no further than the Old Kent Road.   TIM SLESSOR

I was told I was a true cosmopolitan: I am unhappy everywhere.
                                   STEPHEN VIZINCZEY

99 per cent of tourists go to 1 per cent of places, which means that the person you're most likely to see at a tourist destination is another tourist.   GUY BROWNING

Life can take you anywhere you want to go until you get there.
                                   CAROLE MORGAN HOPKIN

When one realises that his life is worth living, he either commits suicide or travels.   EDWARD DAHLBERG

It is a crime to think in Australia.   BETTE MIDLER

What has China ever given to the world? Can you really respect a nation that's never taken to cutlery?   VICTORIA WOOD

There are so many places in the world that, thank God, one need not go to.   D.H. LAWRENCE

ONLY IN AMERICA...

Readers of a sensitive disposition may want to avert their eyes from some of the non-PC quotes contained in the following sections!

* * *

Americans are broad-minded people. They'll accept the fact that a person can be an alcoholic, a dope fiend, a wife beater and even a newspaperman, but if he doesn't drive there's something wrong with him.
ART BUCHWALD

We had a wonderful vacation. Went through five states, ten cities, and eighty-five toll booths.
LEOPOLD FECHTNER

Thanks to the interstate highway system it is now possible to travel from coast to coast without actually seeing anything.
CHARLES KURALT

Get on any major American highway and it will eventually dead-end in a Disney parking area large enough to have its own climate, populated by large nomadic families who have been trying to find their cars since the Carter administration.
DAVE BARRY

In Toronto a teenager was taking her driving test and crashed into six cars while trying to parallel park. She won't be able to drive in Canada, but on the bright side she's just been issued with a New York taxi licence.
CONAN O'BRIEN

In Miami it is not customary to stop for Stop signs. The thinking is: If you do so, the other motorists will assume you're a tourist and therefore unarmed, and they'll help themselves to your money and medically valuable organs.
DAVE BARRY

US Driver identity:

1. One hand on wheel, one hand on horn: Chicago.
2. One hand on wheel, one finger out window: New York.
3. One hand on wheel, one finger out window, cutting across all lanes of traffic: New Jersey.
4. One hand on wheel, one hand on non-fat double decaff cappuccino, cradling cell phone, brick on accelerator, gun in lap: Los Angeles.
5. One hand on 12 oz. double shot latte, one knee on wheel, cradling cell phone, foot on brake, mind on radio game, banging head on steering wheel while stuck in traffic: Seattle.
6. One hand on wheel, one hand on hunting rifle, alternating between both feet being on accelerator and both feet on brake, throwing McDonald's bag out window: Texas.
7. Four-wheel drive pick-up truck, shotgun mounted in rear window, beer cans on floor, squirrel tails attached to antenna: Alabama.

E-TALES

Beverly Hills is so exclusive the Fire Department refuses to make house calls.   WOODY ALLEN

He was driving at 65mph, which in Miami is the speed limit normally observed inside car washes.   DAVE BARRY

I was happy that I could get sixty-five channels on my TV at four in the morning, but I wished there was something to watch other than reruns of *I Love Lucy* and 'infomercials' selling vegetable juicers and sadistic exercise devices.   MARK LITTLE ON A TRIP TO AMERICA

California is a wonderful place. If they lowered the taxes, got rid of the smog and cleaned up the traffic mess, I really believe I'd settle here until the next earthquake.   GROUCHO MARX

In Michigan a mortician who writes poems is the social equivalent of a dentist who does karaoke: a painful case made more so by the dash of dullness.   THOMAS LYNCH

A Texas town has banned the Harry Potter books because they glorify magic. And learning to read.

CRAIG KILBORN

It's a scientific fact that if you stay in California, you lose one point of IQ a year.

TRUMAN CAPOTE

I didn't like LA. The people were rude; I nearly got arrested for smoking in a bar; I was frequently tapped for money by beggars on Venice Beach; a Groucho Marx T-shirt cost $200; and the waiters and waitresses were all out-of-work actors full of bullshit.

ROY 'CHUBBY' BROWN

American men are all mixed up today. There was a time when this was a nation of Ernest Hemingways, REAL MEN. The kind of men who could defoliate an entire forest to make a breakfast fire, and then wipe out an endangered species while hunting for lunch. But not anymore.

We've become a nation of wimps. Pansies. Alan Alda types who cook and clean and 'relate' to their wives. Phil Donahue clones who are 'sensitive' and 'vulnerable' and 'understanding' of their children. And where's it gotten us? I'll tell you where. The Japanese make better cars; the Israelis, better soldiers. And the rest of the world is using our embassies for target practice.

BRUCE FEIRSTEIN

Miami Beach is where neon goes to die.

LENNY BRUCE

If you want to live in America, don't sneak over the border. Do it the right way: Get Angelina Jolie to adopt you.

JIMMY KIMMEL

Las Vegas gets a bad rap. When you think of it you think: gamblers and hookers. It's more of a family place now. It's gamblers, hookers … and their kids.

BARRY MANILOW

The US is like the guy at the party who gives cocaine to everybody and still nobody likes him.

JIM SAMUELS

Bel Air, I'm convinced, was laid out by some diabolic sadist who decided not to use a compass. If you took two dozen cooked noodles and carelessly threw them on a cracked plate, and then threw the whole thing out the window, you'd have a fairly accurate idea of how the roads are laid out.

GROUCHO MARX

It gets so hot in Tennessee, you'd gladly wrap your lips around a trailer hitch if you thought it would drag you north to Canada. Pieces of your thigh stick to the vinyl of car seats there.

RICH HALL

I don't want to move to the Mid-West. I could never live in a place where the outstanding geographic feature is the horizon.

GEORGE CARLIN

Only 11 per cent of the American public bothers to read a daily paper beyond the funny pages or the used car ads.

MICHAEL MOORE

Last year in the US there were more people killed as a result of firearms than car accidents. This trend will continue until we can develop a more accurate automobile.

JONATHAN KATZ

Americans have different ways of saying things. They say 'elevator', we say 'lift'. They say 'President', we say 'Stupid psychopathic git'.

ALEXEI SAYLE

Las Vegas was built for one purpose only: to placate people whilst relieving them of their money.

RICH HALL

Beverly Hills churches are so posh that at communion they offer you a wine list.

BILL POSTON

Americans who travel abroad for the first time are often shocked to discover that, despite all the progress that has been made in the last thirty years, many foreign people still speak in foreign languages.

DAVE BARRY

In California everyone either goes to a therapist, is a therapist, or is a therapist going to a therapist. TRUMAN CAPOTE

I'm not so quick to buy into the premise of the Kennedys being America's Royal Family. Take away the racketeering, bootlegging, gerrymandering, bimbo-wrangling, Mafia liaisons and chronic alcoholism and they're really just the folks next door. RICH HALL

In California you have two IDs – before plastic surgery and after.

ARNOLD SCHWARZENEGGER

America is a place where Jewish merchants sell Zen love beads to agnostics for Christmas. JOHN BRIMER

There are three pastimes in Boston: politics, sports and revenge.

LAWRENCE MOULTER

In some parts of America, ambulances' response times are so slow, the best thing to do is call for a pizza and get the driver to drop you off at the hospital on the way back. DON MACLEAN

I thought San Francisco was drunk but it's an infant sucking in the night compared to Montana. RUDYARD KIPLING

ALL Americans are deaf and blind.

GEORGE BERNARD SHAW TO LADY ASTOR AFTER BEING
INFORMED THAT HELEN KELLER WAS DEAF AND BLIND

I think I know how Chicago got started. A bunch of people in New York said, 'Gee, I'm enjoying the crime and the poverty but it just isn't cold enough. Let's go west.' RICHARD JENI

America is the most litigious nation on earth. People will catch their genitals in zips, then sue the trouser manufacturers. Hence, 'To sue the pants off someone.'   RICH HALL

USA stands for United States of Advertising.   BILL HICKS

Only in America would a guy invent crack. Only in America would there be a guy that cocaine wasn't good enough for.   DENIS LEARY

What's the most popular pick-up line in Arkansas? 'Nice tooth!'   BILL HICKS

In America you're guilty until proven wealthy.   BILL MAHER

American women make excellent ex-wives.   ROMAIN GARY

The air is so rarefied in the Beverly Hills Hotel, you wouldn't be surprised to find it on your bill.   TOM WISEMAN

It is really surprising how many American adults are virtually illiterate, and how very many of them have plunged into psychiatry so that their egos have grown inwards like toenails.   NOEL COWARD

I like Florida. Everything is in the eighties: the temperature, the ages, the IQs...   GEORGE CARLIN

The reason I left Minnesota was because I knew there had to be something more in life besides Walt Disney movies.   BOB DYLAN

I just moved from Boston to LA. Meeting girls is different. In Boston I meet a girl and go 'Wow, what a girl, I hope my friends like her.' Out here it's like, 'Wow, what a nice girl, I hope she's a girl.'   ROBBIE PRINTZ

I've heard the New Jersey jokes but let me tell you, people from New Jersey have great senses of humour. Of course they have to. They're from New Jersey!   ROBERT WUHL

Like so many Americans, she was trying to construct a life that made sense from things she found in gift shops.   KURT VONNEGUT

Every street in LA looks like the road to the airport.   ORSON WELLES

When you become used to never being alone you may consider yourself Americanised.   ANDRE MAUROIS

The average American attention span is that of a ferret on a double espresso.   DENNIS MILLER

I am willing to love all mankind, except an American.

SAMUEL JOHNSON

LA is so celebrity-conscious, there's a restaurant there that only serves Jack Nicholson. And when he shows up, they tell him there'll be a ten-minute wait.   BILL MAHER

American women expect to find in their husbands the perfection that English women only hope to find in their butlers.   SOMERSET MAUGHAM

America is like a beauty contestant. It's gorgeous until it opens its mouth.   RICH HALL

Suburban Chicago is virgin territory for whorehouses.   AL CAPONE

Nobody ever knocked people about like the Americans, to establish the warmth of their own hearts.

JAMES CAMERON

The only difference between crime and business in LA is capital.

RAYMOND CHANDLER

There's nothing wrong with California that a rise in the ocean level wouldn't cure.

ROSS MACDONALD

I have just returned from Boston. It is the only thing to do if you find yourself there.

FRED ALLEN

America is a large, friendly dog in a very small room. Every time it wags its tail it knocks over a chair.

ARNOLD TOYNBEE

I love Thanksgiving turkey. It's the only time in Los Angeles that you see natural breasts.

ARNOLD SCHWARZENEGGER

In America you can always find a party. In Russia the party always finds you.

YAKOV SMIRNOFF

In my experience, American secretaries can make a good cup of coffee, but are not so hot when it comes to dictation, typing or spelling. They also appear to suffer from chronic hay fever the whole year round. They give great telephone, though.

BRYAN FORBES

One of the reasons I love America is because it will give anyone a hearing even if they have no idea what they're talking about.

MARK LITTLE

When the American people get through with the English language, it will look as if it had been run over by a musical comedy.

FINLEY PETER DUNNE

The worst winter I ever spent was one summer in San Francisco.

MARK TWAIN

Unless you're out with the dog, walking in America is something done only by the criminally insane. The common thinking is that if God had meant us to propel ourselves from A to B without resorting to external machinery, he wouldn't have given us wheels, five-speed gearboxes and stomachs which took premium unleaded.

TONY HAWKS

I don't believe in the legend of vigorous youth which America is supposed to represent. More and more she seems to me like the madam of a whorehouse elbowing her way to the bargain counter. When I ride into the bay again and see the old blowser standing in her nightshirt holding aloft the torch of liberty I will simply give her the raspberries.

HENRY MILLER

American water is so dirty, many of our fish are beaching themselves and asking for asylum.

BOB HOPE

My parents didn't want to move to Florida but they turned sixty and it was the law.

JERRY SEINFELD

They have a TV programme in America called *Crimewatch* but you don't have to watch it. You can open the curtains and see it live.

HAL ROACH

To qualify for a Los Angelean you need three things: a driver's licence, a tennis court, and a preference for snorting cocaine.

MICHAEL CAINE

It's an American characteristic not to stop running even after you've arrived.

CLIVE JAMES

In Los Angeles people don't get older – just tighter.   **GREG PROOPS**

I'd rather be a lamp-post in Denver than a dog in Philadelphia.

W.C. FIELDS

In San Francisco now they have a dumb mime group. They talk.

HENNY YOUNGMAN

Americans are crazy people. They treat cigarette smokers like villainous carriers of the Black Death, and yet every home is a virtual arsenal bulging with handguns. Babes from birth suck on the teated muzzles of .38 revolvers and are trained to perforate anyone who might call to the wrong address after nightfall.

HUGH LEONARD

America is the only place I know where they lock up the jury every night and let the prisoner go home.   HARRY HERSHFIELD

Thanks to the miles of superhighways under construction, America will soon be a wonderful place to drive – if you don't want to stop.

FLETCHER KNEBEL

An American is either a Jew or an anti-Semite, unless he is both at the same time.   JEAN-PAUL SARTRE

Fall is my favourite season in Los Angeles, watching the birds change colour and fall from the trees.

DAVID LETTERMAN

I had forgotten just how flat and empty Middle America is. Stand on two phone books in almost anywhere in Iowa and you get a view.

BILL BRYSON

What really got me about America was the plenitude of all-night walk-in taxidermy stores. How convenient.   BILLY CONNOLLY

Life can never be entirely dull to an American. When he has nothing else to do he can always spend a few years trying to discover who his grandfather was.   PAUL BOURGET

Most people move to California so they can name their kids Rainbow or Mailbox, and purchase Swedish furniture without getting laughed at.

IAN SHOALES

The crime situation is so bad in some American cities, you could walk five blocks and never leave the scene of the crime.

E.C. McKenzie

Only Americans have mastered the art of being prosperous and broke at the same time.

E.C. McKenzie

The trouble with Oakland is that, when you get there, it's there.

Herb Caen

The 100 per cent American is 99 per cent idiot.

George Bernard Shaw

Life in Santa Monica is very curious. Every morning a large golden orb appears in the sky. People remove their clothes and jump into pools of water. It is very strange for an Englishman.

Kenneth Tynan

America is engaging in a great orgy of group therapy at the moment in its daytime chat shows. It's like, 'My mother ran away with a giraffe's sister.'

Frank McCourt

All the arts in America are a gigantic racket run by unscrupulous men for unhealthy women.

Sir Thomas Beecham

No one ever went broke underestimating the taste of the American public.

H.L. Mencken

San Diego doesn't look like the kind of town where people get born.

Steve Ellman

Everyone under thirty-five in the US has gone to film school and learned the lingo. They don't think, they just repeat the terrible little slogans.

Orson Welles

The people in Florida like to go to bed early so as they can preserve their energy for lying round the pool the next day.

Con Houlihan

In California they don't throw their garbage away. They make it into TV shows.   WOODY ALLEN

Disneyland can be found in Los Angeles. Wherever you look.

DAVID FROST

You don't die in the United States. You just under-achieve.

JERZY KOZINSKI

Las Vegas is a town dedicated to the proposition that if the greatest thrill in life is to win at gambling, the second greatest one is to lose.

TOM WISEMAN

Nevada has no intellectual life. The members of the divorce colony occupy themselves by playing golf, watching the calendar and practising adultery.   H.L. MENCKEN

Everyone is proud of being a bastard here in Chicago.   SAUL BELLOW

In America you can buy a lifetime's supply of aspirin for one dollar – and use it all up in two weeks.   JOHN BARRYMORE

The food had the neutral aftertaste of the deep-freeze.

JOHN BOORMAN ON
LOS ANGELES CUISINE

America is the world's policeman: a big, dumb mick flatfoot in the middle of the one thing cops dread most: a domestic disturbance.

P.J. O'ROURKE

When you tell an Iowan a joke, you can see a kind of race going on between his brain and his expression.   BILL BRYSON

In Texas we grew up believing two things: God loves you and he's going to send you to hell, and sex is bad and dirty and nasty and awful so you should save it for the one you love.   BUTCH HANCOCK

I like to sit in the cheap theatres of America where people live and die with Elizabethan manners while watching the movies.

RICHARD BRAUTIGAN

It is absurd to say there are neither ruins nor curiosities in America when they have their mothers and their accents.   OSCAR WILDE

THE LAND OF IRE

Visitors to Ireland are fed into our transport system like sausage skins in a pork factory and emerge at the other end Blarney-stuffed.

TONY BUTLER

There's more tar in a packet of fags than there is in the roads of Mayo.

PADRAIG O'CONNOR

A friend of mine, during his occasional dark night of the soul, is much given to declaring that if Ireland is ever given an enema, Roscrea is where they will stick the tube. Personally, I think there are far worse places than Roscrea, a town in which I spent an enchanting twenty-four hours one lunchtime.

HUGH LEONARD

An Irishman is someone who wishes he was somewhere else.

OLIVER ST JOHN GOGARTY

People die here, but they're not permitted to grow old.

HUGH LEONARD ON THE DUBLIN SUBURB OF DALKEY

Belfast is a hard and cruel town inhabited by people who, due to bad planning on the part of whatever passes for a Creator, happen to live next door to each other.

GERRY ANDERSON

If I were asked what I thought would be the national sport of Ireland's future I would say without hesitation – funerals.

ALAN BESTIC

In Ireland we have two of everything. One is the wrong size and the other is due on Wednesday.

HUGH LEONARD

Dublin was a great preparation for Hollywood. It can be a very bitchy, back-stabbing gossipy backwater.

GABRIEL BYRNE

Ireland is a figment of the Anglo-Saxon imagination.

BRENDAN BEHAN

I wanted to play to the bright young Irish – so I came to London.

SEAN HUGHES

I reckon no man is thoroughly miserable unless he be condemned to live in Ireland.   JONATHAN SWIFT

My concern about Ireland's future could be put into the navel of a flea and still leave room for a bishop's humility.   HUGH LEONARD

The people of Northern Ireland have access to the best education system in the British Isles and use it skilfully to turn out maniacs and a disproportionate number of dazed zealots.   GERRY ANDERSON

Navan ... – the only place in Europe that's spelt the same forwards as backwards. That says a lot about it.

TOMMY TIERNAN

If you see an Irishman with a tan, it's rust.   DAVE ALLEN

The definition of Irish Alzheimer's: you forget everything but the grudges.   SEAN KELLY

The greatest investment any Irishman can make is in a good enemy.

SEAN MCCANN

The Irish have spent more time putting the fear of God into men than any other race on earth. If they didn't do it according to the Bible, they did it according to the sword.   SEAN MCCANN

The Irishman's faith in his own perennial poverty is as deep and unshakeable as his belief in the foreigner's eternal wealth.

J.P. DONLEAVY

Ireland is to my mind something like the bottom of an aquarium, with little people in crannies like prawns.   D.H. LAWRENCE

Given the unlikely option of attending a funeral or a sex orgy, the dyed-in-the-wool Celt will always opt for the funeral.   **JOHN B. KEANE**

An Anglo-Irishman only works at riding horses, drinking whiskey and reading double-meaning jokes at Trinity College.   **BRENDAN BEHAN**

Ireland has contributed nothing but a whine to the literature of Europe.
JAMES JOYCE

The typical west of Ireland family consists of a father, a mother, twelve children and a resident Dutch anthropologist.   **FLANN O'BRIEN**

The harp should be replaced by the fiddle as Ireland's national emblem.
BRENDAN MCGAHON SPEAKING OF SOCIAL WELFARE FRAUD IN 1986

Asking an Irishman to write a book about Ireland is like telling a cannibal chief that he must cook his granny for special guests.
ALAN BESTIC

I was brought up in a place called Glenageary, a suburb of south Dublin, where the only exercise anyone ever got was adultery, lawnmowing and going to the shops to buy cheap potent drink in the middle of the day.   **JOE O'CONNOR**

If an Englishman catches a burglar in his house he'll say 'What do you think you're doing?' An Irishman would say 'Get out, you bastard!'
DAVE ALLEN

The quickest way to silence a crowd in a Dublin pub is to say that you are writing a book about Ireland.   **DONALD S. CONNERY**

Ireland is a fatal disease from which it is the plain duty of every Irishman to disassociate himself.   **GEORGE MOORE**

One of the things that has contributed to the idea that women do not exist in Ireland is the fact that when they were first discovered, no one knew what to do with them.   **ANTHONY BUTLER**

The first item on the agenda of every Irish organisation is The Split.

BRENDAN BEHAN

As a born and bred Dubliner, with a lifelong unsentimental but deep affection for the place, I have in the past couple of years come to thoroughly dislike this clogged, short-tempered, loud, greedy, mean-minded, overpriced kip of a city.

GENE KERRIGAN

The damned Irish – they have to moan over something or other, but you never heard of an Irishman starving to death.

ERNEST HEMINGWAY

Dublin used to be one of the prettiest cities in Europe and now it's a shambolical mess.

BOB GELDOF

Northern Ireland has a problem for every solution.

COLIN HENRY

The Irish don't want anyone to wish them well. They want everyone to wish their enemies ill instead.

HAROLD NICOLSON

It makes me nervous to breathe air I can't see.

BOB HOPE ON THE IRISH WEATHER

An Irish alibi is proof that you were in two places at one time.

TONY BUTLER

An Englishman thinks while seated: a Frenchman standing; an American, pacing; an Irishman, afterwards.

AUSTIN O'MALLEY

When I was growing up in Ireland, even spaghetti bolognaise was regarded as exotic food.

DAIRE O'BRIEN

The Irish fight only among themselves. You will never find a gang of them picking on another group because of their colour or race. They would rather knock lumps out of each other. It is the story of the four green fields.

TERRY WOGAN

In most Irish homes there's a terrifying, surreal coloured picture, which appears to represent a doleful hippie ripping his chest open, tacked to every wall. It represents the Sacred Heart of Jesus. Pass no remarks. Frequently it is accompanied by the black-and-white image of a hairy-nosed gaffer, his hands wrapped in bloody bandages. He is Padre Pio. Richard Gere is also popular.   SEAN KELLY

I once met an Irish surfer. These are two words that don't seem to belong together. I asked him how he did it. 'Drunk,' he replied.
                                                              FRANK GANNON

In Bandon, where I grew up, even the pigs are Protestant.
                                                              GRAHAM NORTON

Don't get the idea that the Irish are lax in business. Far from it. When they extract your back teeth you can be sure their next effort will be to sell you a dental plate.   ANTHONY BUTLER

Guilt isn't an emotion in the Celtic countries; it's simply a way of life – a kind of gleefully painful social anaesthetic.   A.L. KENNEDY

I was thinking about the Blarney Stone recently. Only the Irish could persuade people to kiss an edifice the Norman soldiers had urinated on.   DAVE ALLEN

When Irish eyes are smiling ... watch your step.   GERALD KERSH

> Out of Ireland have we come
> Great hatred, little room.
>
> **W.B. YEATS**

You're not a proper member of an Irish club until you're barred.

MICHAEL DAVITT

We Irish have a funny attitude to alcoholism. If somebody tells us they've got cirrhosis of the liver we put out our hands to them and say, 'Well done.'

ARDAL O'HANLON

The Irish jury's decision was unanimous: they sent out for another barrel of Guinness.

HAL ROACH

For God's sake bring me a large Scotch. What a bloody awful country!

CONSERVATIVE HOME SECRETARY REGINALD MAUDLING ON IRELAND AFTER HIS FIRST VISIT TO BELFAST IN 1972

An Irish farmer, to cover the possibility of unexpected visitors, can often be found eating his dinner out of a drawer.

NIALL TOIBIN

I showed my appreciation of my native land in the usual Irish way – by getting out of it as soon as I possibly could.

GEORGE BERNARD SHAW

The Irish wear two contraceptives, to be sure to be sure.

KEVIN MCALEER

If you do somebody in Ireland a favour, you make an enemy for life.

HUGH LEONARD

The true Irish cocktail is made by adding half a glass of whiskey to three-quarters of another.

TONY BUTLER

When passing for Irish, you're advised to go easy on the deodorant and the shampoo. Dandruff is *de rigueur*.

SEAN KELLY

THE SCOTS CLAN

Poor sister Scotland, her doom is fell,
She cannot find any more Stuarts to sell.   JAMES JOYCE

The Scottish are the nymphomaniacs of world rugby.

GEORGE HOOK

There was so much to see in Aberdeen. I can't begin to list it all, but
a highlight was a small tot sitting in the doorway of an estate house
attempting to smash a 9-volt battery with an axe.   RICH HALL

Scottish summers consist of three hot days and a thunderstorm.

JOHN AITON

You know it's summer in Scotland because the rain gets warmer.

TOMMY MCFARLANE

Scotland: land of the omnipotent No.

ALAN BOLD

It is not so much to be lamented that Old England is lost as that the Scotch have found it.

SAMUEL JOHNSON

For a marriage to be valid in Scotland, it is absolutely necessary that it should be consummated in the presence of two policemen.

SAMUEL BUTLER

The noblest prospect which a Scotsman ever sees is the high road that leads him to England.

SAMUEL JOHNSON

The three smallest books in the world are the *British Book of Space Achievers*, *Titalian War Heroes*, and the *Scottish Giftbook*.

ROBERT MCKEE

For Scotland, one should be an amphibian.

D.H. LAWRENCE

Lutherans are like Scottish people, only with less frivolity.

GARRISON KEILLOR

A Scotsman told that it required a surgical operation to get a joke into a Scotsman's head, asked with a puzzled frown, 'And why should you wish to get it in?'   *STRAND* MAGAZINE

The Scots lose their teeth faster than any other community on earth. From the onset of puberty, it seems, their gums long for nudity. If they don't lose their teeth from an excessive intake of sugar, they go along to the Celtic-Rangers matches and get them knocked out instead.

GWYN THOMAS

The Scottish media are a bunch of unreconstructed wankers.

TONY BLAIR

They say that if an Irishman is blessed with the ability to talk, he's kissed the Blarney Stone. They say that if an Englishman is blessed with the ability to talk, he's a politician. They say that if a Scotsman is blessed with the ability to talk, he's sober. **DAVE ALLEN**

To the Bank of Scotland I bequeath my testicles, because it has no balls. **LORD ERSKINE**

Like many Scottish men, my father loved all things bad for him.
RHONA CAMERON

The reason all Scots have a sense of humour is because it's free.
BOB MONKHOUSE

If you gave a Scotsman poison, he wouldn't die until he'd recovered the deposit on the bottle. **LES DAWSON**

When a boy is bored with Glasgow he is ready to live. **IAN PATTISON**

A Scotsman would have asked for separate cheques at the Last Supper. **LES DAWSON**

As far as I'm concerned, Scotland will be reborn when the last minister is strangled with the last copy of the *Sunday Post*.

TOM NAIRN

The state of deprivation in Glasgow is appalling. There's a waiting list of two years to vandalise a phone box. **ARNOLD BROWN**

WELSH RAREBITS

What do you call a Welshman with more than one sheep? A bigamist.

MILES JEFFREYS

Finding out your sister is black is fine. Finding out she's Welsh is another thing entirely.

A.A. GILL

It's a scientific fact that the Great Wall of China and the Welsh sense of national outrage are the only two earthly things visible from outer space.

ANTHONY TORMEY

When you come from Wales you're a f***ing man. We take pit ponies and put a bit of rubber hose pipe in their mouth and drag them into the sea to wash the grime off them. We're tough in Wales.

RICHARD BURTON

Not everyone in Wales looks benignly on cultural pursuits. There is a suspicion of art's loftier reaches. I am reminded of the Swansea councillor who snorted, 'Ballet? Ballet is just a leg show for the nobs!'

TREVOR FISHLOCK

When she called him a Welsh bastard he was offended, but he didn't say which of the two words hurt him most.

JOE O'GORMAN

I went to Wales once but it was closed.

BOB MONKHOUSE

This bloody land is full of Welshmen.

DYLAN THOMAS

The Welsh remain the only race you can vilify without being called a racist.

A.N. WILSON

Wales is forever associated with inedible salad.

GRIFF RHYS JONES

I love it when Welshmen tell jokes. It stops them singing for a few minutes.

BILL SHIPTON

Everyone goes into the pub sideways and the dogs piss only on back doors, and there are more unwanted babies shoved up the chimneys than there are used French letters in the offertory boxes.

DYLAN THOMAS ON THE WELSH VILLAGE OF LLANGAIN IN 1944

There are parts of Wales where the only concession to gaiety is a striped shroud.

GWYN THOMAS

Wales is very sparsely copulated.

DOUGLAS HOME

The Welsh people have lived in a permanent state of emergency since about 383 A.D.

GWYN WILLIAMS

Would anyone notice if Wales disappeared, except for people in the West Country, who would then own seaside homes?

PAT FITZPATRICK

The Welsh are insistent that Welsh names must not be pronounced as they are spelt.

JOHN TICKNER

The Welsh are so damn Welsh that it looks like affectation.

SIR ALEXANDER RALEIGH

FRENCH TOASTS

There is no hell. There is only France.

FRANK ZAPPA

France has neither winter nor summer nor morals but apart from these drawbacks it is a fine country.

MARK TWAIN

A French writer has paid the English a very well-deserved compliment. He says they have never committed a useless crime.

PATRICK PEARSE

She was on the phone from the Riviera. 'The holiday is wonderful, darling. I feel like a new woman.' 'So do I,' her husband replied, 'Stay another week'.

GEORGE COOTE

When God created France he realised that he'd gone overboard in creating the most perfect place on earth. So to balance it out, he created the French.

MITCHELL SYMONS

Paris is like a whore. From a distance she seems ravishing, you can't wait to have her in your arms. But five minutes later you feel empty, disgusted with yourself. You feel tricked.

HENRY MILLER

It's no accident that *debacle* is a French word.

JOHN LANCHESTER

The French are tremendous snobs, despite that rather showy and demonstrative Revolution.

ARTHUR MARSHALL

You can't go to Paris any more. It's not there.

JACK GILBERT

The French invented the only known cure for dandruff. It's called the guillotine.

P.G. WODEHOUSE

The ignorance of French society gives one a rough sense of the infinite.
JOSEPH RENAN

It is important to remember that the French have always been there when they needed us.
JOHN F. KENNEDY

Since it is now fashionable to laugh at the conservative French Academy, I have remained a rebel by joining it.
JEAN COCTEAU

If the French won't buy our lamb, we won't use their letters.
GRAFFITO

In France we threaten the man who rings the alarm bell and leave him in peace who starts the fire.
SEBASTIEN CHAMFORT

A blaspheming Frenchman is a spectacle more pleasing to the Lord than a praying Englishman.
HEINRICH HEINE

English physicians kill you whereas French ones just let you die.
LORD MELBOURNE

A Frenchman is an Italian with a bad temper.   DENNIS MCEVOY

It is unthinkable for a Frenchman to arrive at middle age without having both syphilis and the Cross of the Legion of Honour.

ANDRE GIDE

Britain has football hooligans. Germany has neo-Nazis – and France has farmers.   THE TIMES, 1992

God, what on earth was I drinking last night? My head feels like there's a Frenchman living in it.   BEN ELTON

ITALIAN STALLIONS

'When you sailed around Italy, did you touch Florence?' 'No, my wife
wouldn't let me dare.'   DANNY CUMMINS

I went to Venice once and got seasick crossing the street.
                                                         JASPAR CARROTT

It's against the law to look attractive in your passport photo unless you
have an Italian one.   GUY BROWNING

Pwll: So you're not going to Venice this year?
Tym: No, it's Vienna we're not going to. It was Venice we didn't go to
          last year.   WYNFORD JONES

I love the way Italians park. Turn any street corner in Rome and it looks
as if you've just missed a parking competition for blind people.
                                                         BILL BRYSON

Naples is a city that combines the vice of Paris, the misery of Dublin
and the vulgarity of New York.   JOHN RUSKIN

Not for nothing is Rome known as the Eternal City. It takes an eternity to
get anything done there.   JOHN GREGORY DUNNE

Did you know that over a hundred roadsweepers a year are drowned in
Venice?   KEN DODD

Let's be frank. The Italians' technological contribution to humankind
stopped with the pizza oven.   BILL BRYSON

Italian men have to make sure you know they've got a penis.
                                                         W.H. AUDEN

The reason the Romans built their great paved highways was because they had such inconvenient footwear.   **Montesquieu**

Italy is a country of 55 million actors, the worst of whom are on the stage.   **Orson Welles**

Margaret Thatcher only went to Venice because someone told her she could walk down the middle of the street without having to worry about cars.   **Neil Kinnock**

Gina Lollobrigida is the most publicised aspect of Italian life since Nero stopped throwing Christians to the lions.   **Tom Wiseman**

A country as devoted to the condom as Holy Communion.
Pól Ó Conghaile on Italy

The Italians invented birth control. They call it garlic.   **P.J. O'Rourke**

Rome is a very loony city. One only needs to spend an hour or two there to realise Fellini makes documentaries.   **FRAN LEBOWITZ**

Italian men dance as if they want to make love to you and drive as if they want to kill you.   **DORIS LILLY**

Sicilians love having their children photographed by any passing stranger, and will offer to dress them up in their ugly bests for you to snap.   **NORMA LORIMER**

THE REST OF THE EUROPEANS

Look at the situation the Swiss have got themselves into. They've got the French to the left of them, the Austrians to the right, the Germans up above and the Italians down below. You'd never sell that flat, would you?

AL MURRAY

The best that can be said for Norwegian television is that it gives you the sensation of a coma without the worry and inconvenience.

BILL BRYSON

The Polish army has just bought 10,000 septic tanks. When they learn how to drive them they're going to invade Russia.

LARRY WILDE

Always check foreign change while your hand is still out. Nine times out of ten it will be correct but it's always worth checking for 20ps from Guernsey, which seem to be that island's largest export.

GUY BROWNING

The only way to tell the difference between German wine and German vinegar is by the label.

MARK TWAIN

Never shoot a film in Belgrade. The whole town is illuminated by a 20-watt light and there's nothing to do. You can't even go for a drive. Tito is always using the car.

MEL BROOKS

One of the main troubles about going to Europe is that no one wants to hear about your trip when you get home. Your friends and relatives are rife with jealousy and are not only sorry that you went to Europe, but deeply regret that you came back.

ART BUCHWALD

If It's Tuesday, This Must Be Belgium. **FILM TITLE**

Life is too short to learn German. **RICHARD PORSON**

The time to enjoy a European trip is about three weeks after unpacking. **GEORGE ADE**

Poland is a place where, if Bo Derek walked along the street in nothing but shoes, people would look at her shoes first.

JOHN GUNTHER

I don't like Norway. The sun never sets, the bar never opens, and the whole country smells of kippers. **EVELYN WAUGH**

My family was entirely Nordic – which is to say, idiots.

HENRY MILLER

It's untrue that all Germans are bad drivers: they hit everything they aim at. **JOEY ADAMS**

Malta is the only place in the world where the local delicacy is the bread. **ALAN COREN**

If you have a stomach ache in France you get a suppository. In Germany you go to a health spa. In the United States they cut your stomach open and in Britain they put you on a waiting list.

PHIL HAMMOND

The German language sounds better when you're speaking it with a stroke.

KIRK DOUGLAS

What a bloody country Switzerland is. Even the cheese has holes in it.

TOM STOPPARD

The Greeks were nothing more than impoverished descendents of a bunch of la-di-dah fruit salads who invented democracy and then forgot how to use it while walking around dressed up like girls.

P.J. O'ROURKE

I speak Spanish to God, Italian to women, French to men, and German to my horse.

CHARLES V

The Germans never live from their real feelings, only from the ones they invent in their heads. And that's why, as a bourgeois crowd, they're so monstrously ugly.

D.H. LAWRENCE

Every window gleams like silver. Every brass knob looks like polished gold. If a loose piece of paper fell into the street the mayor would probably lose his job.

JOHN FANTE ON COPENHAGEN IN 1957

A man can read Goethe or Rilke in the evening and go to his work at Auschwitz the following morning.

GEORGE STEINER

I don't think Europeans make better films. In fact they can't even keep their johns clean.

PETER FONDA

Poland has managed to greatly improve its lifestyle thanks to the introduction of certain modern Western conveniences – like food.

DAVE BARRY

A gifted person ought to learn English in thirty hours, French in thirty days, and German in thirty years.

MARK TWAIN

I'm starting a campaign to have Finland removed as a country. We don't need it.

GEORGE CARLIN

Continental people have a sex life. The English have hot water bottles.

GEORGE MIKES

The food in Yugoslavia is fine if you like pork tartare.

ED BEGLEY JR

Beer is the Danish national drink, and the Danish national weakness is another beer.
CLEMENTINE PADDLEFORD

Waiting for the German verb is surely the ultimate thrill.
FLANN O'BRIEN

Since both its natural products, snow and chocolate, melt, the cuckoo clock was invented by Switzerland in order to give tourists something solid to remember it by.
ALAN COREN

I once thought about killing myself but went to Belgium instead.
STEPHEN FRY

Norwegian food is noticeably inferior to Swedish, though after we left Oslo it stopped tasting as if it had been made with the milk from porcupines.
MARGARET HALSEY

If you strip a Spaniard of all his good qualities he becomes a Portuguese.
HESTER THRALE

I always feel you can do Europe in a wheelchair.
ERMA BOMBECK

Anyone who goes to France votes Conservative. Anyone who goes to Italy votes Labour, and anyone who goes to Spain has, at some point in the recent past, held up a post office.
JEREMY CLARKSON

THE REST OF THE WORLD

In Pakistan a judge sentenced a convicted murderer to be strangled, cut into 100 pieces and thrown into a vat of acid for his crimes. And that was a plea bargain.

COLIN QUINN

A Canadian is someone who drinks Brazilian coffee from an English teacup and munches a French pastry while sitting on his Danish furniture, having just come from an Italian movie in his German car. He then picks up his Japanese pen and writes to his local MP to complain about the American takeover of the Canadian publishing business.

CAMPBELL HUGHES

Many people are surprised to hear that we have comedians in Russia. We do, except they're all dead.

YAKOV SMIRNOFF

Toronto is like New York run by the Swiss.

PETER USTINOV

A nest of papacy where Irish troops and Roman bastards can disport themselves unchecked.

SAMUEL PEPYS ON TANGIER

The best thing about Hawaii was leaving it. I found the beauty a bit bloody tiresome, and missed the cold drabness of the UK. There's only so much sunshine and rainbows a man can tolerate. When it's sunny all the time it's a bit weird. There's no *Eastenders*, there's no gin, and there's nobody going 'Fack Off'.

RUSSELL BRAND

Sao Paolo is like Reading, only much farther away.

PETER FLEMING

In Seattle you haven't had enough coffee until you can thread a sewing machine while it's still running.

JEFF BEZOS

In 1733 the Russian army had a treatment for soldiers who suffered severe homesickness. At the first sign of the condition they buried the soldier alive. That's good. I like people who go right to the heart of a problem.   GEORGE CARLIN

Australia is like Arkansas with a beach.   GREG PROOPS

The whole complexion of the modern world is due to the absence from Jerusalem of a lunatic asylum.   HAVELOCK ELLIS

All the drinks in Hawaii have something floating in them. It's kind of like our water back in Los Angeles.   BOB HOPE

The Japanese have perfected good manners and made them indistinguishable from rudeness.   PAUL THEROUX

I don't remember much about Nairobi but I know I was there because it says so on my passport.   MALACHY MCCOURT

There are two reasons we shouldn't buy Korean cars. The first is because Koreans eat dogs. And the second is because they're crap.
                                                                JEREMY CLARKSON

My generation of Canadians grew up believing that, if we were very good or very smart, or both, we would some day graduate from Canada.   ROBERT FULFORD

Northern Ireland is like Beirut only without the Christians.
                                                                ADRIAN WALSH

Poor Mexico: so far from God and so near the United States!
                                                                PORFIRIO DIAZ

Ireland will put a shillelagh into orbit, Israel will put a matzo ball into orbit, and Lichtenstein will put a postage stamp into orbit before the Canadians ever put up a mouse.   BRENDAN BEHAN

Q. Why doesn't Mexico have an Olympic team?
A. Because all the Mexicans who can run, jump and swim are already in the US.

INTERNET JOKE

Russia has gone from communism to gangsterism without a second's pause for capitalism.

MITCHELL SYMONS

In Mexico everything on the menu is the same dish. The only difference is the way it's folded.

BILLY CONNOLLY

If Jesus wept over Jerusalem He must be heartbroken over Sydney.

FRED NILE

Pakistan is the sort of country to send your mother-in-law to.

IAN BOTHAM

The boat ride to Africa is so long, there are still slaves on their way there.

CHRIS ROCK

Cusins is a very nice fellow. You'd never guess he was born in Australia.

GEORGE BERNARD SHAW

A Scotsman on holiday in Iraq was giving directions to a friend on how to get to his hotel. He said, 'It's situated about ten miles on the Glasgow side of Baghdad.'

DES MACHALE

It is not without its significance that bungee-jumping was invented in New Zealand, a land of scenery, sheep and suicide. Suicide can never be far from the minds of most thinking New Zealanders. I suppose bungee-jumping is the closest they can get.

TERRY WOGAN

Toronto will be a fine city when it's finished.

BRENDAN BEHAN

I was over in Australia and I was asked, 'Are you proud to be an American?' I was like, 'I don't know. I didn't have a lot to do with it. My parents f***ed there. I hate patriotism. Instead of putting stars and stripes on our flags we should put pictures of our parents f***ing.

BILL HICKS

Home advantage counts for little in Luxembourg soccer matches. The corners have to be taken from well inside Belgium.

ANDY LYONS

The Russians love Brooke Shields because her eyebrows remind them of Leonid Breznev.

ROBIN WILLIAMS

If Moses had been a committee, the children of Israel would still be in Egypt.

DICK CAVETT

Sodom was a church picnic and Gomorrah a convention of girl scouts compared to Tangier, which contained more thugs and degenerates than any place I've ever visited.   **ROBERT RUARK**

Chopsticks are one of the reasons the Chinese never invented custard.   **SPIKE MILLIGAN**

Jews don't drink much because it interferes with their suffering.

MILTON BERLE

The Russian police have a Missing Persons Department. That's where they decide which persons are going to go missing.

YAKOV SMIRNOFF

You can tell Australian hamburgers by the way the meat starts eating the lettuce.   **JOHNNY CARSON**

Very little is known of the Canadian country since it is rarely visited by anyone but the Queen and illiterate sport fishermen.   **P.J. O'ROURKE**

Why is psychoanalysis quicker for Aussies? When it's time to go back to their childhood, they're already there.   **DAN GREENE**

A riddle wrapped in a mystery inside an enigma.
WINSTON CHURCHILL ON RUSSIA

There's been another revolution in South America. But then it's Tuesday, isn't it?   **EAMON NALLY**

Canadians are cold so much of the time that when they die many of them leave instructions to be cremated.   **CYNTHIA NELMS**

Australians are among the few people in the world who consider a pot belly a status symbol.   **DENNIS OAKLEY**

The high-rise buildings in Auckland have all the architectural appeal of Shane MacGowan's teeth.   **RICH HALL**

The shapes of countries have always fascinated me. Laos is a dead ringer for Lisa Simpson.   **RICH HALL**

You can't even get a parachute to open in Melbourne after 10 p.m.
MAX BYGRAVES

I shouldn't be in Canada at all. My ancestors made a terrible mistake. But I have to keep coming back to Montreal to renew my neurotic affiliations.   **LEONARD COHEN**

If it has four legs and isn't a chair, if it has two wings and flies but isn't a plane, and if it swims and isn't a submarine ... the Cantonese will eat it.   **PRINCE CHARLES**

The Faroe Islands only have a population of 172 – and nine of those are sheep.   **PAT DOLAN**

There are seventy verses in the Uruguay national anthem, which fact may account for the Uruguay standing army.   **FRANKLIN P. ADAMS**

To live in Australia permanently is rather like going to a party and dancing all night with one's mother. **BARRY HUMPHRIES**

Chiba is a concrete city. Unbroken, charmless concrete. The place has been reclaimed from the sea, and if the sea had any decency at all it would claim it back. **TOM HUMPHRIES**

I shook hands with a friendly Arab. I still have my right hand to prove it. **SPIKE MILLIGAN**

Realising that they will never be a world power, the Cypriots have decided to be a world nuisance instead. **GEORGE MIKES**

I can't have any respect for a country whose evolution stopped with the moose. **TOMMY TIERNAN ON CANADA**

Blackpool is the English Siberia. **KENNETH WILLIAMS**

I once heard a Californian student in Heidelberg say, in one of his calmest moods, that he would rather decline two drinks than one German adjective. **MARK TWAIN**

Inside every fat Englishman there's a thin Hindu trying to get out. **TIMOTHY LEARY**

Chernobyl looked nice in the brochure. **VICTORIA WOOD**

Other titles published by The History Press

Submariners News
The Peculiar Press of the Underwater Mariner
KEITH HALL

In this entertaining book, author Keith Hall examines the development of this strange branch of 'underwater journalism', collating the articles and anecdotes, jokes, cartoons and stories that have been published over the years to brighten up the lives of submariners far from home, providing an insight into their bizarre self-contained world.

978-0-7524-5793-2

Signal Box Coming Up, Sir!
And Other Railwaymen's Stories
GEOFF BODY AND BILL PARKER

This entertaining collection of railwaymen's experiences presents genuine situations and incidents that occurred over the last fifty years. It embraces a great variety of humorous anecdotes, from daring robberies, footplate adventures, animal capers and mishaps, to unusual lines and summer madness – these are just a few of the subjects retold in this assortment of memorable experiences by professional railwaymen.

978-0-7524-6040-6

Glamour in the Skies
The Golden Age of the Air Stewardess
LIBBIE ESCOLME-SCHMIDT

Glamour in the Skies is packed with anecdotes ranging from administering oxygen to passengers flying over the Andes, to serving French champagne on Concorde. Covering sexual discrimination, disasters, glamorous stopovers and other temptations, this book records the changing times in air travel through the eyes of the stewardess and offers the perfect tribute to the girls who walked the skies.

978-0-7524-5787-1

Has Britain Gone Bonkers?
CHRIS MARTIN

If you dream of a country without caravans, where people are free to hunt foxes, smoke in pubs and where the Health and Safety Executive has been disbanded then this is the book for you. Speed cameras, ramblers, people carriers... our country is going down the toilet and nobody in power seems to care – what can be done to make Britain great again?

978-0-7524-5711-6

Visit our website and discover thousands of other History Press books.
www.thehistorypress.co.uk